Promoting Mental, Emotional and Social Health

Schools are now seen as being one of the key agencies that can help redress society's most fundamental problems, create more cohesive communities and promote citizenship and a sense of social conscience in the young. Though keen to respond, schools are already under so many pressures that such responsibilities can seem daunting.

Promoting Mental, Emotional and Social Health: A Whole School Approach provides a clear and practical overview of ways in which mainstream schools can promote the health of all those who work and learn in them. Supported by the latest new evidence from the UK and Europe, as well as findings from the USA, it outlines and examines:

- evidence that social and emotional learning and academic achievement can go hand in hand, and that the same key factors underlie both happy and effective schools
- the areas of school life that are the key to promoting social and affective health, including relationships with families and the community, management and the curriculum
- the competences that we all need to become more emotionally literate and relate more effectively to others.

Promoting Mental, Emotional and Social Health: A Whole School Approach will prove invaluable to all teachers interested in knowing how social and emotional education can help schools manage their everyday concerns.

Katherine Weare is Director of the Health Education Unit at the University of Southampton. Her previous publications include *Developing Mental and Emotional Health in the European Network of Health Promoting Schools* for the World Health Organisation.

Promoting Mental, Emotional and Social Health

A Whole School Approach

Katherine Weare

London and New York

First published 2000 by Routledge
11 New Fetter Lane, London EC4P 4EE

Simultaneously published in the USA and Canada
by Routledge
29 West 35th Street, New York, NY 10001

Routledge is an imprint of the Taylor & Francis Group

© 2000 Katherine Weare

Typeset in Sabon by Taylor & Francis Books Ltd
Printed and bound in Great Britain by St Edmundsbury Press, St
Edmundsbury, Suffolk

British Library Cataloguing in Publication Data
A catalogue record for this book is available from the British Library

Library of Congress Cataloging in Publication Data
Weare, Katherine, 1950–
   Promoting mental, emotional, and social health: a whole school
   approach / Katherine Weare.
   p. cm.
   Includes bibliographical references (p.) and index.
   1. School children–Mental health. 2. Schools–Sociological aspects.
   I. Title.
   LB3430.W42 2000
   371.7'1–dc21   99–16832
   CIP

ISBN 0–415–16875–9 (hbk)
ISBN 0–415–16876–7 (pbk)

Contents

Acknowledgements

I would like to thank the World Health Organisation (WHO) and, in particular, Erio Ziglio, David Rivett, Vivian Rasmussen and Heather Macdonald for involving me in work on mental and emotional health in the context of the European Network of Health Promoting Schools (ENHPS), which proved a valuable seedbed for trying out some of the ideas that shaped this book with professionals involved in school education across Europe. Thanks to the WHO again, and to David Stears and Carl Parsons of the Centre for Health Education Research at Christ Church University College, Canterbury, for their permission to use some of the case studies from their evaluations of the ENHPS as illustrations in this book. Thanks to my graduate students and colleagues in the Health Education Unit, Research and Graduate School of Education, at the University of Southampton for being a sounding board for some of these ideas, especially to Jenny McWhirter for her kind help in finding materials, Jonathan Shepherd for his patient help with searching the literature and Karen Ragan for keeping track of it all. Thanks particularly to three people who read drafts of the book: my colleague and friend, Gay Gray, with whom I have worked for many years on these issues and whose wise advice has helped me with the formulation of my ideas, my friend and fellow teacher, Sue Tarlton, who inspired me to realise how vital these matters are in practice and, most of all, my husband, Barry Lunt, who gave me copious personal and practical support to make the writing of the book a reality, somewhat at the expense of his own mental, emotional and social health.

Introduction
Why promoting mental, emotional and social health is becoming a fundamental issue in schools

Goals of this chapter

This chapter provides a brief overview of work that is emerging from a variety of fields that are coming together to create a new interest and focus on mental, emotional and social health, and suggests some reasons why schools should become more involved in this area.

The new emphasis on mental, emotional and social health

The traditional low status of work in this area

Mental, emotional and social health has long been the 'poor relation' in all the disciplines that are concerned with it: in psychology, health promotion, education and the health service, the area has never been well-resourced or taken as seriously as other issues. In education, for example, work on mental, emotional and social health issues has mostly been focused on pupils of lower abilities, or those seen as troublesome or troubled (Bender 1987), rather than being seen as of relevance to the whole school community, to 'normal' pupils or to teachers. It has also been more likely to be seen as important in primary than in secondary schools, and has suffered from going in and out of fashion. In the UK, for example, considerable progress was made in introducing health, personal and social education into the school curriculum in the 1970s, but unfortunately its presence was then reduced by the introduction in the late 1980s of the National Curriculum. Health education, and personal and social education, were not made part of the core curriculum, but were the subject of 'guidance' documents only (Buck and Inman 1992): as a result many schools have felt under too many other pressures to give these areas the attention they often know they deserve.

However, despite its low status, useful work has long existed on mental, emotional and social health in many different fields. Such work is now being supported by new research and practice from several different disciplines, which are coming together to demonstrate the importance of this issue in new and dynamic ways, creating a new interest in social and affective health in schools. The reasons for the shift in emphasis and importance are various, and we outline some of the most significant ones below.

The new biology

The nineteenth and early twentieth century were keen to emphasise the difference between man and animals, and focus on 'man as a rational being', at the apex of the tree of evolution, rising above his animal origins. The logical conclusions of Darwinism, with its emphasis on man as an animal, took some time to have a real impact on our understanding of what it is to be human, but in the late twentieth century a certain disillusionment with the notion of progress, civilisation, rationality and industrialisation has lead to an interest in ecology and environmentalism that has caused us to recognise, acknowledge and even celebrate our links with the rest of creation rather than our differences. This shift of perspective is suggesting that our emotions are perhaps the most fundamental part of what it is to be human. We have come to recognise that the root emotions, such as fear, anger or joy, are instinctive, biological responses, which have been essential to the survival and progress of the human race, to outside events. Feminist thinking has contributed to this change as feminist thinkers have found it easier to acknowledge the importance of instinct and emotion to human life.

In learning to accept the centrality of the emotions, we are also coming to appreciate that there is today an overwhelming need to manage them. As society has changed, the intensity of the negative emotions, especially anger and fear, is now not so useful, and our basic physiological response to threat of 'fight or flight' is no longer an appropriate response to most modern problems. Without the physical challenges that allowed our ancestors to discharge strong emotions we are often left in a state of stress and tension, which causes us to be depressed, anxious or hostile. We need to help ourselves and others understand and cope with feelings, and find productive rather than destructive ways to use them. For most of us this takes a great deal of effort, but it is one to which schools need to devote themselves if they are to help us become more fully human and civilised.

The breakdown of social structures

In terms of human survival, managing our emotions and our social relationships is perhaps the single most important challenge that faces the human race. Internationally and nationally, wars and violence continue to rage while the threat of war blights the lives of many people. Understanding and reducing these threats are to a large extent a matter of understanding and managing individual, group and mass emotion. Nations and factions may occasionally be driven to war and violence to right wrongs, but negative emotions such as fear, hatred, intolerance, suspicion, greed for territory, and the need to identify with their own group by demonising another are more usually the root cause. If it is to prevent the horrors of war and violence, humankind needs to learn a great deal more about controlling basic emotions and finding peaceful ways to negotiate and solve conflicts.

In terms of our own personal and social survival the need for us to manage our emotions and understand our fellow human beings has never been more pressing. Most societies are experiencing an increase in mental illness, crime (including violent offences), drug abuse and divorce. People have become more isolated from each other. We are seeing a breakdown in communities and in traditional patterns of employment, and an increase in urban alienation, with people increasingly living as lone individuals or small families, locked away behind their doors. The breakdown of the extended family and the rise of a more mobile population have meant that the nuclear family has become the main focus of social cohesion, and the support of any larger community has become less significant. As a result of the increase in social fragmentation, young people no longer have the same number of adult role models to which to turn, and many grow up in one parent families and are likely to have absent fathers, while a sizeable proportion spend some or all of their young lives in the care of the authorities with no long-term parents to call their own.

Increased pressure on the young

At the same time as young people are being deprived of meaningful support, they are being faced with increased demands and challenges. The world in which young people are growing up today is very different from the world their parents inhabited when young, and they are facing an accelerated pace of social change that would have been unfamiliar, even to those who grew up a decade ago. Furthermore, young people are being forced to grow up much faster than did previous generations and no longer experience much of a protected stage of childhood: through television and other media they are increasingly exposed to adult ways of thinking, experience, problems and pressures in ways that they may well not be equipped to handle. Young people often have significantly different values and attitudes to those of adults – a generation gap that makes it hard for adults and young people to understand each other, which can be a source of anxiety for adults and uncertainty for the young.

Many young people have become alienated from the political process, and feel they have no voice in their own community, let alone in wider society. As a result of social fragmentation and the alienation of the generations, the peer group has become ever more powerful as perhaps the only source of social support and reference for many young people. Those who do not readily fit in with the peer group may find themselves isolated or, worse, the focus of bullying. But even for those that do fit in, some peer groups may be a source of danger if the youth culture involved is the kind in which dangerous lifestyles, such as the taking of hard drugs, violence and crime, or other risk-taking behaviour has become the badge of acceptance.

There is overwhelming evidence that increased social pressures are taking their toll on the mental and emotional health of everyone, especially the young. Young people are suffering from various forms of mental distress to a quite extraordinary and probably unprecedented extent. A British House of Commons select committee estimated that 10–20 per cent of young people will experience a mental health problem serious enough to require professional help during the course of their lifetime (Mind 1997). In the UK, one-third of younger teenagers claim to feel currently 'stressed' or 'depressed' (Gordon and Grant 1997), while in the US, 60 per cent of girls and 40 per cent of boys had suffered from 'depressed episodes' by the time they reached their older teens. Globally the number of successful suicides, especially among young men, has risen steadily since the early 1980s (DoH 1992), while attempted suicides have risen even more, especially among girls (Coleman 1997). Meanwhile, young people often help create rather than alleviate their own problems: bullying, for example, is a current cause of fear for one in three young people in the UK (Balding 1998).

In response to these multifaceted social and personal problems, many are coming to see schools as being one of the key agencies that, in liaison with the home and with a range of other community and national agencies, can help redress a range of society's most fundamental problems: from war and violence (Lantieri and Patti 1996; WHO 1998c) to the creation of more cohesive communities and the promotion of citizenship (Hawkins and Catalano 1992) to the discovery of a sense of purpose, values and social conscience in the young (Kessler 1997).

Effective schools affect mental, emotional and social health

Schools may feel that such calls for action are yet another unrealistic pressure, and one to which they do not have the time to respond given the other demands on them. To date the practical thrust of the currently fashionable school effectiveness movement has been academic performance in the traditional, core curriculum subjects, measured by standardised tests of attainment and by public examination results. Many teachers feel themselves to be more than fully occupied in meeting ever-spiralling external requirements, and curriculum time for what are sometimes seen as 'softer' areas has therefore been even more undermined. Furthermore, the increasing emphasis on performance, league tables and school accountability is undermining schools' motivation to manage pupils who are having social and emotional difficulties: there is evidence that slower and more troublesome pupils who threaten to dilute school results through their poor achievements or who are taking up what is seen as too much valuable time are being neglected (Kelly 1997) and excluded in greater numbers than before (Smith 1998).

It is vital that those who seek to promote high academic standards and those who seek to promote mental, emotional and social health realise that they are on the same side, and that social and affective education can support academic learning, not simply take time away from it. There is overwhelming evidence that pupils learn more effectively, including their academic subjects, if they are happy in their work, believe in themselves, like their teachers and feel school is supporting them (Aspey and Roebuck 1977; Hawkins and Catalano 1992; Goleman 1996; McCarthy 1998). The influences work both ways, and it is clear that achievement in school in academic subjects is of vital importance to pupils' happiness and self-esteem (Gordon and Grant, 1997).

Intelligence is 'multiple' and can be emotional and social

Teachers could take heart from realising that work in social and affective health can support their efforts to teach the academic curriculum. The importance of satisfying emotional and social needs before people can concentrate on matters of the intellect has long been recognised (Maslow 1970), and recent work in psychology is coming to see humankind's intellectual, social and emotional sides as parallel and equal rather than hierarchically arranged. Gardner's work on 'multiple intelligences' (Gardner 1993a 1993b; Gardner *et al.* 1995) has been highly persuasive and influential in demonstrating that there are many different and equally valid ways to be 'intelligent'. He argues that to limit our definition of intelligence to the cognitive and intellectual is to be far too restrictive and narrow, and results in giving everyone an education that is only appropriate for the few who go on to an academic career. He has identified seven separate intelligences – two of which he has classified as the 'personal intelligences'. One of these, 'intra-personal intelligence', he defines as the ability to understand oneself, to form an accurate model of oneself and use it to operate effectively in life. The other, 'interpersonal intelligence', is the ability to understand others, how they work, what motivates them and how to work cooperatively with them. Gardner suggests that we need to pay more attention and respect to these forms of intelligence, seeing them on a par with more traditionally accepted types of intelligence, such as logical and spacial.

There is evidence that the different types of intelligence support each other, and indeed that intellectual forms of intelligence cannot operate without emotional intelligence. We have known for some time that people cannot think clearly when in the grip of powerful feelings, especially negative ones (Weissberg and Elias 1993) and that long-term, chronic emotional problems make people unable to learn effectively (Goleman 1996). But there is increasing evidence that emotional and social intelligence and cognitive and intellectual intelligence not only influence one another but are fundamentally inseparable (Sylwester 1995), and that social and emotional competences are essential for the successful development of intellectual and cognitive processes (Brendtro *et al.* 1990; Perry 1996). So the emotions are coming to be seen as a part of, not the enemy of, rationality. Mayer and Salovey (1997) suggest that emotional intelligence is essential to our ability to think clearly: by directing our attention towards what matters, the emotions help us to prioritise, decide, anticipate and plan. Our key life decisions are too important to leave to the intellect alone: without the value that emotion attaches to outcomes there is no way of deciding which outcome is 'better', and all decisions can seem equally good (Damasio 1994).

So to suggest that schools should concentrate more on social, emotional and mental health is not simply to add yet another demand to a teacher's already impossible workload; effective social and affective education is directly beneficial to academic attainment, and can therefore help teachers be more effective in meeting the many demands they face.

New demands on teachers

Teachers certainly need all the help they can get. Teaching has always been challenging: every teacher in their working day plays a wide range of roles, including public speaker, actor, learning facilitator, curriculum planner, classroom manager, counsellor, mediator, social worker, friend and surrogate parent to name but a few. These roles demand a vast range of capacities, which are as much emotional and social as they are intellectual and technical, and the effective teacher has always had to possess a high degree of emotional and social competence and maturity.

On top of these traditional demands teachers are now facing a range of new challenges, and increasingly need help to develop the capacities to rise to them (Johnstone 1992). The pressures on the young are making them more difficult to teach: they are not only more depressed but also more disruptive, less likely to accept authority without question or to see the sense of schooling in a time of high unemployment. The rise of a multicultural society means that teachers need to have a much wider appreciation of a broad range of social, cultural, ethnic and religious backgrounds, and the ability to relate sensitively to people whose assumptions and practices may be new to them.

Teachers are under increasing pressure to be seen to perform. Classrooms and schools are no longer 'secret gardens' in which individual teachers have autonomy: schools are now much more accountable to those from outside who subject them to relentless and very public scrutiny and evaluation. At the same time as they are under increased pressures, schools are being asked to take more responsibility for their own management, with a decrease in the kinds of support that used to be provided by the local authority and less help from increasingly underfunded agencies, such as the school psychological service.

Invariably such increased and diverse demands on teachers are leading to a rise in stress-related illness and absenteeism, a decrease in morale, difficulties in teacher recruitment and a rise in the teacher drop-out rate (Leech 1995; McEwen and Thompson 1997; Kyriacou 1996).

So, at a time of great change, teachers are very much in need of the practical, psychological and social supports to help them cope. This support includes receiving the kind of professional development that can help them to develop their own emotional and social capacities and coping skills – both to respond effectively to new challenges and to have the personal and professional esteem to resist assertively demands that they see as unreasonable or inappropriate (Hall *et al.* 1997).

Mental, emotional and social health as the 'missing piece'

The teaching profession is no longer held in the high esteem it once was, and teachers are often blamed for society's ills, with all the misdemeanours of the young – from bad manners to hooliganism to drug taking – being laid at their door. Schools have increasing social expectations placed upon them: whenever there is a moral panic in society, schools tend to be put forward as the answer not only to traditional problems, such as low literacy and numeracy, but to newer concerns, such as racism, sexism and teenage violence. (In some senses, of course, this book can itself be seen as another example of such growing expectations, although it is hoped that the suggestions it provides will prevent it from being seen as yet another set of onerous demands.)

Again, teachers can gain support from social and affective education. It is usually the case that the issues that are of current concern to the educational community, which are, at the time of writing, teacher recruitment and retention, the prevention of school failure, teenage violence, bullying, racism, drug abuse and teenage pregnancy, are in essence mental, emotional and social health issues. Many who have worked in this area see affective and social education as the 'missing piece', the generic key to all the rest of our more detailed educational and social concerns (Shriver and Weissberg 1998; Elias 1997). If schools and indeed society could get this right, the rest would be more likely to follow.

The importance of emotions and relationships to health

Schools are increasingly being asked to become more involved in health education, and many are doing so. Although the emphasis in school health promotion still tends to be on physical health and on teaching specific topics, such as drug avoidance, nutrition and exercise, there is a growing realisation that mental, emotional and social health need to be far more prominent (Stewart-Brown 1998), and that a concern with physical health should be underpinned by a concern with emotional and social matters.

It is clear that the emotions affect our physical health directly. People who experience negative emotions for long periods are much more prone to illness. There is overwhelming evidence that anger appears to be particularly bad for the heart and that high levels of hostility at an early age double the risk of heart attack in middle age (Williams 1989), while the sense of having no control over one's job also appears to be linked to heart disease (Marmot *et al.* 1997). Depression impedes recovery and makes death more likely (Goleman 1996), which may be because depression, grief, stress and anxiety lead to a suppression of the immune system, and hence to illnesses such as colds and flu (Glaser and Kiecolt-Glaser 1987; Seligman 1991). So helping people to manage their emotions and relate effectively to others is without doubt a direct form of disease prevention.

Our feelings and our relationships also affect our physical health more indirectly, as the origin of most health-related behaviour is to a large extent emotional and social. People choose to look after their health, or not, partly as a result of how they feel about themselves, for example, whether they think they are worth looking after, whether they believe anyone cares about them and whether they believe that they can change (Becker 1984; Wallston and Wallston 1982; Seligman 1991). People are motivated to take care of the health of others according to how they feel about the family, group or community they are in and their place within it (Adams and Smithies 1990; Graham 1984). So, effective school health education must have a concern with the emotional and social roots of health-related behaviour at its heart.

The changing nature of work

Schools have always seen at least part of their function as being preparation for work, and in many countries this role is receiving an increased emphasis. The nature of work has changed dramatically in the last half of the twentieth century, and several factors have combined to make social and emotional competence at least as important as technical skill to work-related performance and success. The shift from manufacturing industries to service industries in many developed countries has meant that work has become increasingly social rather than technical, and has brought about an increased emphasis on communication, teamwork, self-motivation and human management. The increasing rate of change in types and patterns of employment means that people need to be self-motivated, flexible, adaptable and know how to learn, rather than being wedded to a particular profession for life. The onset of rapid personal communications has meant that few of us now work in isolation, but have to adjust rapidly to interacting with many different people in a day, using a range of media.

Given the increasingly social nature of work, it is therefore not surprising that the evidence shows that emotional and social abilities are fundamental to success in life. Many different studies have shown that abilities such as emotional resilience, getting on with others, handling frustrations and managing emotions are a far better predictor of career success at work than is IQ (Valliant 1977; Felsman and Valliant 1987). Interestingly, such attributes have also been shown to be a better predictor of academic and scholastic success than IQ, tests of knowledge or reading scores (Mischel and Peake 1990; Hawkins and Catalano 1992). So, if they seriously wish to fulfil their role in vocational preparation effectively, it is clear that schools need to expand their vision from a concentration on intellectual, cognitive and factual aspects of learning to pay much more attention to teaching the emotional and social competences that the modern workplace demands.

Intrinsic reasons

Finally, we might consider that work in this field may need no extrinsic justification, but has a logic and a face value to the ordinary citizen that may elude some academics and politicians. It is reasonable to propose that we should educate about mental, emotional and social health because it is intrinsically a worthwhile thing to do. Achieving happiness, emotional balance and good relationships are 'good things' in themselves, and need no further justification, although there are many such justifications as we have seen.

Many people spend most of their time and money in, sometimes misguided, attempts to find happiness by seeking a job or career they find fulfilling, a partner with whom they are compatible, friends who understand them and leisure pursuits that help them relax and enjoy themselves. The growing attraction of practices such as meditation, which focus on calm and inner peace, would suggest that many people are increasingly proactive in this search for emotional fulfilment, and realise the need for some education and guidance in this most crucial of personal tasks.

Conclusion

There are then a great many reasons why schools should engage with mental, emotional and social health. And the good news is that if they do, it works. There is overwhelming evidence that people can learn the knowledge, skills and attitudes that help them to get on with each other better, to be physically, mentally, emotionally and socially healthier and to be happier. There is evidence too that some social environments are much more conducive to social and affective health than others. This book explores the evidence for the importance of social and emotional education, and the principles and practices that are starting to make its promotion a reality in our schools.

1 Definitions, concepts and principles

Goals of this chapter

This chapter provides a keynote and a guide to the rest of the book. It examines the nature of mental, emotional and social health, suggests that we need a framework of concepts and principles for examining these matters, and that the approaches of health promotion in general and the health promoting school in particular are currently the most coherent, comprehensive, ethically sound and well-proven. The concepts and principles that underlie health promotion and the health promoting school idea are set out, their relevance to social and affective health in schools suggested, and indications given of where they will be explored in more detail in the chapters that follow.

Choosing and defining terms

Mental/emotional/social

It may help at this early stage to make some observations about the choice of the three terms – mental, emotional and social – which frame the book. At first sight it may seem tautological: almost all definitions of mental health include emotional well-being, and for some the two are simply synonymous, while most definitions of mental health also include social well-being, as the ability to make relationships and be part of a social group are generally seen as essential to mental health. In theory, then, this book could have just used the term 'mental health' on the grounds that it subsumes the other two terms. The reasons not to restrict ourselves in this way are pragmatic rather than conceptual, and are to do with the way the terms tend to be used in practice.

The book uses the term 'mental health' in order to speak to those people who come to these issues from the health service, health education, health promotion, and international agencies such as the WHO, who tend to use this term, often in a broad, positive and holistic sense. But although many who use the term in these contexts strive to give it a positive spin, mental health tends so often in practice to be used as a synonym for mental illness that to use it on its own would be too narrowing and negative for the more positive orientation of this inquiry. Furthermore, the term 'mental health' does not conjure up for those from educational backgrounds the wealth of work that exists in their field, which takes place under the labels of emotional, social or personal education, but which is in fact central to mental health. Nor does it have helpful connotations to those who come from the worlds of therapy and counselling, for whom the term often has an overwhelmingly psychiatric and medical colouration. So the book also uses the term 'emotional health', not to distinguish it from mental health, but simply because it is a term more often used by those who come to the issue through mainstream school education and the therapeutic professions. It adds the term 'social health' because it is a familiar one to educators and also to those who come to these issues from work in the community. Using the term 'social health' also has the advantage of making it clear from the outset that the focus of this book is not on the individual, but also on social aspects of mental health. It reminds us, for example, that the mental and emotional health of individuals depend on the social support they receive, that communities can be more or less healthy, and that the concepts of mental and emotional health are not neutral and obvious, but are to some extent socially defined and contextualised.

Mental health is too complex to define simply

We will begin by making some comments on the problems of definition, and will for now, for simplicity's sake, focus only on the term 'mental health', partly because that is the more inclusive term, and partly because it is one that a good deal of effort has been devoted to defining. So there are several issues with which we must deal.

   This book will not attempt a single-sentence definition of mental health: most who have made a serious attempt to define it have concluded that to attempt to sum up such a complex and multifaceted concept in a short, simple statement is just not appropriate or possible. Those who have tried end up either coming up with something pithy but so banal as to be meaningless, or inclusive but so packed with nouns as to be impossible to follow. Many who tackled the problem have concluded that it is more helpful to suggest a range of elements (Macdonald and O'Hara 1998) or descriptions (HEA 1997) that constitute the concept. But saying that we need to use a multifaceted approach does not mean that we should attempt to define mental health as a 'shopping list' of disconnected attributes and features: such approaches have rightly been described as reductionist and atomistic (Secker 1998) and give no guidance as to which approaches are to be preferred to others.

Mental health depends on the perspective or paradigm

In deciding how to define mental health we need first to decide what are our basic assumptions and values. Exploring the concept of mental health can never be a culture-free or morally and ethically neutral activity (Caplan and Holland 1990; Tudor 1996). What we understand by mental health will depend on our values, preconceptions and assumptions, for example about the nature of health and illness, the nature of society, the place of the individual within society, what constitutes normality, desirable behaviour and attitudes, and so on. Tudor (1996) has identified four different basic 'paradigms' in the field, all of which lead to quite different definitions of mental health and goals for mental health promotion. So we need to recognise that mental health is socially constructed and socially defined: different professions, communities, societies and cultures have very different ways of conceptualising its nature and causes, determining what is mentally healthy, deciding what interventions are appropriate, and so on. We need not conclude from this, however, that mental health is so socially contextualised that it is impossible to define or explore, and that one paradigm is as good as any other: to do so is to collapse into an unhelpful state of relativism. It is also to misunderstand the theory of the populariser of the concept of paradigms, Kuhn (1962), who suggested that new paradigms succeed earlier ones not just because they are held by more powerful groups, but also because they fit and work better by providing a more comprehensive and convincing account of what is known about the world. But we do need to be aware that all statements we read about mental health come from a particular perspective, even if the originator is not consciously aware of this, and be reflective and explicit ourselves about the assumptions and values behind any approach we propose.

To date most work in mental health has been dominated by the health services; in particular the medical, psychiatric and psychological professions. Without wishing to disregard the humanistic and radical perspectives that have often been taken by some who work in these fields, health service approaches, on the whole, tend to have a particular slant. They tend to focus on illness not health, to conceptualise mental health and illness as an individual rather than a social issue, and to see understanding and action on mental health as properly emanating from professionals 'on top' rather than from lay people 'below'. If we wish to challenge such assumptions, we need a different framework which starts from different premises, which makes sense of the concept in a coherent, holistic, practical and ethically sound way, as well as fitting the available evidence.

A coherent and ethical framework

WHO *concepts and principles*

The WHO, and several academic theorists and professional practitioners, have spent the last fifteen years or so developing an ethically sound set of principles for health promotion, which makes explicit the values and assumptions on which they are based, and which provides a coherent, well-developed and evidence-based framework for thinking about what is potentially an overwhelmingly complex and highly contentious area. Through the work of the WHO, and others at the forefront of the field, health promotion has been able to bring the different issues and perspectives of a wide range of other disciplines together in a highly effective and practical way (Bunton and Macdonald 1992). This book will apply these key concepts and principles to the promotion of mental, emotional and social health in schools. The desirability of this approach is justifiable not on ethical and ideological grounds alone: it stands up to empirical testing too, as we shall see in the course of the book.

Applying a health promoting framework to mental, emotional and social health in schools will be largely unexplored territory, although there are many partial maps to guide us. Health promotion as a framework is only just starting to be applied to mental heath promotion (Tudor 1996; Macdonald and O'Hara, 1998; HEA, 1997; Secker, 1998), and has not yet been systematically applied to mental health in schools. Until very recently, work in mental health has been fairly isolated from developments in the wider field of health promotion. There has generally been a singular lack of communication between health promotion and the theory and practice of mental health, the origins of which operate in both directions. It has been caused partly, as we have said, by the individualistic perspective on mental health taken by the health professions, and also by a lack of identification by those working in schools with the medicalised and rather frightening term 'mental health'. But those working in health promotion have contributed to the rift by tending to use obscure jargon, and, in their concern to promote the wider vision, not always taking into account the needs and constraints of the professions with which they deal or linking with the frameworks and terminologies the professions use. Much seminal work in health promotion is published in official documents and specialist academic textbooks that are hard for practical professionals to access. Even parts of the WHO itself have not made the links, and the global Division of Mental Health appears somewhat to restrict itself to its vision of mental health promotion in schools to the teaching of psycho-social skills (Bosma and Hosman 1991; Lee 1994) without reference to the wider concepts of health promotion used by the health promoting school that is being developed in other parts of the WHO.

So, in exploring what we mean by mental, emotional and social health and their promotion in schools we will attempt to show how the sometimes abstract concepts that inspire heath promotion can be brought alive and applied in the context of schools, and to link the terminology and concepts of health promotion with the language and issues of education.

Using 'the health promoting school' as a framework

Just as the WHO concept of health promotion is considered by those at the forefront of the discipline to be the most useful one for understanding mental health in general, so health promotion and, in particular, the 'health promoting schools' idea is considered by many of those who have devoted much effort to considering the issue to be the most useful framework for exploring health promotion in schools. Health promotion and the health promoting schools idea have been applied as a core perspective to a range of issues in schools right across the world and its breadth has proved to be supportive of and compatible with other frameworks (Elias *et al.* 1996) and adaptable to a wide range of cultures (Rowling 1996; WHO 1998a). Given that mental, emotional and social health are also generally considered to be at the heart of school health promotion, it was surely only a matter of time before an effort was made to apply a health promoting school framework to them. The need for a holistic framework to make sense of this field has already been recognised, and other frameworks such as 'emotional literacy', 'conflict resolution', 'problem solving', 'social competence' and 'community building' have all been used with some success, and this book will most certainly make use of the considerable body of work they have inspired. But none of these frameworks is as comprehensive, as adaptable and as ethically sound as the health promoting school idea. So, while recognising that the health promoting school concept is by no means the only framework that has been used to provide coherence in this field, we suggest that it has more to offer than any other, and we therefore use it as an overall perspective within which the contribution of other disciplines, perspectives and frameworks will be located.

The European Network of Health Promoting Schools

Regional networks of health promoting schools can now be found throughout the world (WHO 1998a) especially in the western Pacific region, Australia and North America (St Leger 1999). Perhaps the most conceptually sound and best-evaluated manifestation of the idea, and one that has given it a notable level of official support, is the European Network of Health Promoting Schools (ENHPS).

The ENHPS is funded by the European Union and the Council of Europe, and managed by the WHO, who have provided a core team to lead it and whose philosophy and principles, derived originally from the Ottawa Charter, officially underpin it (WHO *et al.* 1993; McDonald and

Ziglio 1994). Some forty European countries, in eastern and central as well as western Europe, including (separately) England, Wales, Scotland and Northern Ireland, have joined the ENHPS since 1992 in a series of staggered starts. Over 500 schools are now directly involved in the network, with a further 2,000 able to participate through specific national arrangements. The Network has been heavily supported by international development meetings, by research and by education for coordinators and teachers from schools, including a teacher education project on mental and emotional health (Weare and Gray 1994). The Network has been subjected to systematic evaluation across Europe (Piette 1995; Parsons *et al.* 1997) and within countries (HEA and NFER 1997a), the results of which are now being published. This book will therefore be one of the first easily available commercially published texts to be able to include examples of work in promoting mental, emotional and social health that has resulted from work within the ENHPS – examples that can start to provide a balance to the vast amount of work on social and affective education that has come from the US.

The first conference of the ENHPS at Thessaloniki in Greece in 1997 (WHO 1997a) brought almost all of the coordinators of the Network together. It summarised the key values and principles that underlie the health promoting school concept, namely positive health, empowerment, democracy, equity and partnerships with communities, and emphasised the importance of the school environment, the community context, the curriculum, teacher education and evaluation – all issues that this book will explore.

There has inevitably been something of a rift between theory and practice, even in committed ENHPS schools (Nutbeam 1992). In the UK, in particular, some ENHPS schools have reported that they find the holistic ideal to be out of touch with their everyday realities and constraints, and some schools have proved to be uncomfortable with some of the more radical principles such as democracy (HEA 1995a). It may be that other countries have had similar difficulties, and not had the opportunity to report them, but on the whole the ENHPS would appear to have been a greater success in other parts of Europe than the UK. So if we are to retain the term 'health promoting school' and its central concepts and principles, and link them with other educational and social initiatives, it is imperative that the health promoting school idea should be made clearly relevant to the everyday context of schools in the UK and elsewhere.

With the need to make the discussion relevant and appropriate to schools very much in mind, the next sections make some attempt to define mental, emotional and social health within a health promoting framework.

Defining mental, emotional and social health within a health promotion framework

Mental, emotional and social health can be positive

Work that describes itself as being about 'mental health', especially in the context of the health service, usually turns out on examination to be concerned solely with mental illness, while work described as 'mental health promotion' very often turns out to be restricted to the prevention of mental illness. Similarly, work that describes itself as health promotion in schools sometimes focuses only on the prevention of problems of individual pupils, such as depression, drug abuse, anti-social behaviour and unwanted pregnancy. In so far as schools have taken a whole school perspective on mental, emotional and social health, they sometimes tend to focus on the prevention of problems, such as violence, bullying and conflict.

It is however possible to have models of mental health that are more than euphemisms for its alternative, and models of emotional and social health that promote wellness in individuals and positive practices and relationships in organisations. Given its well-known definition of health as 'a complete state of physical, mental and social well-being, and not merely the absence of disease or infirmity' (WHO 1946), which has stood for over half a century now, the WHO has always preferred to take an approach that starts from a positive basis, sometimes called the 'salutogenic' or wellness model (Antonovsky 1987). For example, the Ottawa Charter suggested that health is 'a positive concept, emphasising social and personal resources, as well as physical capabilities' (WHO 1986).

If we apply a positive, salutogenic perspective to mental, emotional and social health, we shift the focus from mental illness and emotional and social problems alone to include positive well-being. Within this perspective, the promotion of mental, emotional and social health is more than the prevention of mental illness and social and emotional problems, important though that may be. It includes, for example, increasing people's degree of happiness, vitality, sense of self-worth, sense of achievement and concern for each other. In the school context, education for mental, emotional and social health becomes not just about preventing unhappiness, bullying, violence and conflict, it also becomes about encouraging all who learn and work in schools to achieve their goals, to love, to feel joyful, energetic, full of life and to care about others.

Mental, emotional and social health promotion includes the prevention of problems

Taking a salutogenic approach does not preclude a concern with preventing illness and problems: the two are perfectly compatible. Some involved in health promotion, especially in the UK and Europe, have ideological problems with the concept of prevention, seeing it as tending to encourage the use of a top down, atomised and 'medical model'. Some take the view that it is very difficult to include complex, positive perspectives within a preventive framework, or to focus on emotional and social health (Stewart-Brown 1998). However, it is clear if we look at work in the US on mental, emotional and social health promotion in schools, that the concept of 'prevention' does not necessarily constitute such a barrier. For example, an extremely useful series of reviews of programmes by Durlak and colleagues (1995, 1997) is labelled as 'preventive' and also manages to incorporate a very broad range of issues and whole school solutions, including social and community initiatives and those that focus on social and affective health. So this book will include a concern for prevention as part of its goals for the promotion of mental, emotional and social health.

Health as a continuum or spectrum

We may be able to cut through the hoary old arguments about health or illness by agreeing with the many who have suggested that rather than constantly trying to draw dividing lines between the well and the ill, it is preferable to conceptualise health and illness as a continuum. To apply the well-known tripartite framework of 'levels of prevention' to mental health (Tones 1981), at the 'tertiary' level we have established an incurable mental illness, where the goal can only be to manage and control the problem. At the 'secondary' level we have temporary mental illness or strain from which a person can hope to return to wellness. At the 'primary' level we have those who are 'well' and wish to stay that way, and at this level an almost infinite range of mental, emotional and social states is possible – from just coping with life, trudging joylessly along through daily tasks, to the ultimate, and very rare, state of perfect contentment and joy in which we tackle life's challenges with boundless vigour and energy, and feel at one with ourselves, with others and with the universe. Most people, of course, including those who would classify themselves as 'well', move to some extent along this continuum at different times in their lives.

More recently, some have suggested that to think in terms of one continuum is too simplistic, and that we need to conceptualise mental health and illness as being on two separate continua (Trent 1992) so that it is, for example, possible to be diagnosed as mentally ill, but also possible to experience positive mental health and well-being. In the context of our present concerns with mental, emotional and social health it may be even more helpful to break mental health and illness down into a range of different continua, for example into their emotional and social dimensions, so that it is possible, for instance, to be diagnosed with a mental illness such as schizophrenia, but also possible to enjoy positive emotional health, or be a depressive, but socially well-integrated person. Others have suggested that the 'linear' concept of the continua is in itself too restrictive, and that we need to see various aspects of health and illness as distinct but overlapping concepts (Downie *et al.* 1990), or as a spectrum with degrees of health and illness co-existing across a range of dimensions, which include, for example, mental, emotional, physical, social and ecological dimensions (Cribb and Dines 1993).

Whatever model we prefer, the general principle of seeing the relation-ship between illness and health as a matter of degree, not kind, is highly useful in keeping matters in perspective. It reminds us that mental, emotional and social problems are common to us all, not just to a deviant and/or sad minority, and that those who have problems will probably recover, and in any case are not defined by their problem, but almost certainly have a good deal that is positive in their lives. Most of us experience mental, emotional and social health problems at some time – being all subject to the kind of stresses, strains, loneliness, grief and uncertainty that can lead us to feel depressed, withdrawn or confused, to engage in anti-social behaviour or to seek solace in some kind of addiction or dependency. All schools experience disruptive behaviour, conflicts, bullying, violence and a wide range of other social and interpersonal difficulties; those that claim they do not are either exaggerating or are unaware of what is happening in their midst. Most people, and most schools, also have a wide range of strategies, capacities and social supports to help them cope with these problems.

In any case, experiencing minor mental and emotional health problems can be viewed as a necessary part of healthy development: Withers (1995), in a major review of programmes for at-risk youth in the US, Canada, Australia and the UK, concluded that all adolescents feel anger and frustration, and experience a range of temperamental disturbances due to the many physical, emotional and social stresses associated with their developmental stage. Experiencing emotional or cognitive problems is not necessarily a sign of ill health, nor are mentally healthy people always happy. It is often highly appropriate to feel sad, angry, persecuted or confused (Wilberg 1998). Getting in touch with these feelings, under-standing them, acting on them, resolving them and moving on is very much part of the process of learning and maturation – a process, as we shall see, in which schools can facilitate.

It is, however, also important not to use the need to take a relativistic perspective as a reason to be complacent about mental and emotional distress and social problems. We need to recognise that a very considerable number of us will be so disabled by our moods and our experiences that we and others around us may see ourselves as 'ill'. Mental illness is rightly a large and growing area of concern all over the world. The WHO estimate that clinical psychiatric disorder now constitutes over 10 per cent of the total burden of disease worldwide and is due to rise to over 15 per cent by the year 2020, and that globally as many people die of suicide as of road accidents (Harvard and WHO 1996).

Serious mental health problems are common in schools too: in 1997, Young Minds, the leading mental health charity for young people, estimated that in the UK the average secondary school of 1,000 pupils will at any one time contain 50 students who are clinically depressed, a further 100 in significant distress, and 10 affected by eating disorders, while 5–10 of its pupils will attempt suicide in the next year (Mind 1997). Social problems in schools are also very widespread: a major national survey in the UK showed that half of all young people reported having been bullied at some time at school, one in five of them during the current term (HEA 1999). Bullying can have very serious consequences – nearly half of a sample of adults who were bullied as children say they contemplated suicide while still at school, and many say that the experience still has lasting impact on their lives (Kidscape 1998). Recognising that mental, emotional and social problems are common does not mean we do not need to take them seriously, quite the reverse.

The inclusive and relativistic perspective suggests that we should not ghettoise mental, emotional and social health: the principles behind helping those in trouble are applicable to all. As Graham and Rutter (1970) suggest, rather than seeing people who have mental and emotional problems as qualitatively different from those who do not, it may be more helpful to recognise that there is no 'type' of person who gets into emotional difficulties or causes trouble for others, it could be anyone, including ourselves. The promotion of mental, emotional and social health is for everyone, not just for the few with present problems. However, to date, the majority of work in the field of mental health has been concerned with the needs of troubled and troublesome pupils, those with special needs and emotional problems, and those whose problems disrupt the school community. Although this book most certainly includes such pupils in its concerns, and will explore the wealth of work that has attempted to help them, this work will be put into perspective within a broader and more positive focus on mainstream schools, on the whole school population and on teachers as well as pupils, not least because the processes which help some have been shown to help all (McMillan 1992; Cohen 1993; Rutter *et al.* 1998). The strategies that will be suggested are intended to help those in current difficulties, prevent future problems, enhance the positive mental, emotional and social well-being of all who work and learn in schools, and produce supportive environments in which all can positively thrive.

Mental health is fundamentally social

Health promotion is essentially a social discipline: by definition it focuses on the wider structures and actions that promote health rather than just restricting itself to the individualistic focus of health education. Thinking through the implications of this social focus has been the major preoccupation of those working on concept formation in the discipline for the last fifteen years. A key event in the evolution of this social concept, the Ottawa Charter (WHO 1986), set out five areas for action to promote health, three of which were social and structural – they were 'developing healthy public policy', 'the establishment of supportive social and natural environments' and 'community action'. The Charter was highly influential in moving forward our understanding of how to shift the focus of health promotion away from the health attitudes and practices of individuals alone to include a holistic concern with developing 'supportive social and natural environments' often summarised as the 'healthy settings' approach (WHO 1991; Dean and Hancock 1992). The settings approach recognises that health is the product of a myriad of interconnected and interacting physical, social and psychological factors. It attempts to shape a total context where not only the physical environment but the surrounding ethos and relationships provide a climate that is supportive to health. If we take this approach to mental, emotional and social health, we no longer focus only on the needs of individuals, but on the kind of environments that support or undermine social and affective health.

The school as a setting

The settings approach has given rise to several related initiatives, including 'healthy cities', 'healthy hospitals' and, most significantly from our point of view, 'health promoting schools' (WHO 1998a). Applying the settings approach to schools has led to a broadening of the traditional concerns of health education, which have long been with the curriculum and the individual pupil, to one in which the totality of school life is examined, understood and mobilised (St Leger 1999). The health promoting school approach attempts to shape the whole school context, including the school's ethos, organisation, management structures, relationships and physical environment, as well as the taught curriculum, so that the total experience of school life is conducive to the health of all who learn and work there. Looking even more broadly, the school is seen as part of its wider community, reaching out to, and supported by, parents, local health services and other agencies, and involving them in programmes and interventions that support the efforts the school is making to promote health (Nutbeam *et al.* 1991; Pollack 1991).

The school setting is then essentially holistic or, as some now label it, 'eco-holistic' to reflect the interrelated nature of the parts and the whole (Parsons *et al.* 1997). Many are now concluding that mental, emotional and social health must be at the heart of the concept, for example, the twelve WHO 'criteria for a healthy school' (HEA 1999: 5) start with three that are directly linked with mental, emotional and social health – being 'the active promotion of self-esteem of all pupils', 'the development of good relations' and 'the clarification ... of the social aims of the school' (many of the other nine are also indirectly linked with this issue).

So this book will take an eco-holistic, settings approach to the promotion of mental, emotional and social health in schools. The familiar focus on the development of competences in individuals through the taught curriculum will be there, but located within a wider vision of the school as a complex environment, linked with its wider community. Suggestions for action will be concerned with strengthening the supporting environment in a range of ways, not just through teaching and learning, important though they undoubtedly are, but also through management, relationship building, the school ethos, professional development, and communication between the school and outside agencies.

The need to address structural and political problems

Traditional work on mental health promotion has focused on individuals' attitudes and beliefs, which are seen as underlying their lack of mental health, for example, attitudes such as 'low self-esteem', 'external locus of control', 'fatalism' or 'short-term hedonism'. However, the social focus of health promotion has reframed this concern, and suggests that to focus only on individuals and their 'dysfunctional' attitudes is to 'blame the victim', and not tackle the root causes of ill health, which are social and structural (Rodmell and Watt 1986). The attitudes individuals have can certainly create difficulties, but we need to see them as symptoms as well as causes, and recognise that they may well represent realistic assessments of the position in which the less powerful find themselves (Mitchell 1984). We cannot change attitudes unless we change the contexts that gave rise to them.

This means that, as well as working with individuals, we need to address social problems that are the root of mental and emotional health problems. These problems are inevitably deep-seated, structural and political in nature, and include poverty, social inequality, racism, oppression and discrimination (Townsend *et al.* 1992). Tackling these structural problems is seen as a central goal for schools that are serious about wanting to promote the health of all their pupils, controversial though this requirement clearly is for some schools (HEA 1995a). The Thessaloniki conference on the ENHPS included 'equity' among its core principles for the health promoting school, a principle which it said 'guarantees that schools are free from oppression and discrimination, fear and ridicule [and] provides equal access to all to the full range of educational opportunities' (WHO 1997a: 35).

This book will therefore examine ways in which schools can tackle some of the root causes of mental, emotional and social ill health. Chapter 2 will look at the need for schools to become more socially inclusive by tackling their own discriminatory attitudes and practices, by meeting the needs of special needs and difficult pupils, and by encouraging participation from parents and all other sectors of the local community. But it has to be recognised that, in comparison with the individually focused, competency building work we shall examine next, socially focused work is much more difficult, challenging and contentious, and there is nothing like the same number of examples to report or to build on (Secker 1998; St Leger, 1999).

Personal dimensions of mental, emotional and social health

The social and the individual perspective complement one another

We have said that the Ottawa Charter suggested five areas for action, three of them social. However, in our enthusiasm to promote the social it is important to remember that there were also two others, namely 'the enhancement of the individual with the knowledge, skills and motivation to make competent decisions about their health', which is entirely concerned with individual change, and 'the reorientation of the health services to health promotion', which is also partly about individual change in the behaviour, attitudes and values of those who attempt to deliver health. So the Charter recognises that we must not neglect the need to build the capacities of the individual.

It is in fact impossible fundamentally to change social structures without changing the hearts and minds of the individuals who inhabit them; unless we change attitudes and values, new arrangements will simply revert to recreating the conditions they were supposed to replace. For example, if we want schools to be more open and democratic, it is not enough to ask schools to put school councils in place; we need also to educate teachers to cope with the transfer of control, and to educate pupils and parents to have the skills to participate responsibly and effectively if the new arrangements are to be sustained. Promoting social change and promoting individual change should not then be seen as being in opposition: they are two sides of the same coin. Many look at how the social and the personal interplay with one another by examining, with what the Mental Health Foundation (1999) called 'risk and resilience' factors, the complex social and personal features that promote or demote mental health (Macdonald and O'Hara 1998).

So the next section will outline the dimensions of mental, emotional and social health that are concerned with the capacities of individuals, and will indicate where the book will deal with them. In tackling these issues we will find much to draw on as most work on mental, emotional and social health has focused on individuals, and the field is well-developed, conceptually and empirically.

Personal competences are complex and active

In the interests of clarity this section will explore the facets of personal competency separately, but it is worth bearing in mind that few in the field would conceptualise them this way. Most would bring a range of competences together in complex statements, for example:

> Social and emotional competence is the ability to understand, manage and express the social and emotional aspects of one's life in ways that enable the successful management of life tasks such as learning, forming relationships, solving everyday problems, and adapting to the complex demands of growth and development.
>
> (Elias *et al.* 1997: 2)

Looking at the competences separately can also make them seem rather passive, a series of inner states, thoughts and feelings, when those who attempt to promote personal competences would emphasise that they are in need of demonstrating and acting out if they are to become what health promoters now often term 'action competences' (Bruun Jensen 1994, 1997; WHO 1997a). Competences need to be put into practice to empower people to change their own personal behaviour and feelings, and change the social context in which they find themselves. It is often not until the competences come together, for example a sense of self-esteem combined with an ability to make relationships, that we are able to take action to demonstrate our competence and change our circumstances. So, when examining the various personal dimensions of mental, emotional and social health, we need to bear in mind that these dimensions are not in practice usually conceptualised or operationalised in these separate forms.

Self-esteem

A sense of positive self-esteem is almost universally viewed by those who have studied human development as the foundation of health in general, and mental, emotional and social health in particular. A lack of self-esteem has been shown to lead to problems with other key personal capacities and competences, such as unassertiveness, self-criticism and a sense or powerlessness, and thus results in stress and psychological problems (Macdonald 1994). For many, self-esteem forms part of their core definition of what it is to be mentally healthy: for example, Jenkins, McCulloch and Parker define mental health as 'a belief in our own worth and the dignity and worth of others' (1998: 5), while Macdonald and O'Hara see it as 'feeling that you have rights, feeling worthy, feeling you have power and can control and influence your experiences in the world' (1998: 9). In recognition of its fundamental importance, Chapter 3 in particular will spend some considerable time exploring the issue of self-esteem, its complexities and controversies, and how schools can best promote it.

Emotional well-being

There is strong consensus on the centrality of emotional well-being to mental health, and a considerable body of work on emotional education in schools which tends to take for granted what we mean and understand by the concept. However, defining mental health as emotional well-being proves to be deceptively simple. We may perhaps all agree that one of the goals of mental health promotion is helping people to experience positive emotions such as happiness, calmness or joy more often, but after that the picture is confused and contentious. There is considerable disagreement about the role of negative emotion – whether it is simply an irritation to be suppressed and overcome or viewed as a barometer of underlying problems that need addressing, or seen as a valid experience in its own right to be understood and fully experienced (Wilberg 1998). There are different views too on whether the goal of emotional education is control or expression. There has been a massive amount of work, particularly in the US, on how we can teach people to understand their emotions intellectually and get them under control (Goleman 1996), perhaps paradoxically because in the US uncontrolled emotional self-expression, especially in the young, has rather got out of hand. But the taken-for-granted goal of emotional control is beginning to be challenged by those from psycho-therapeutic backgrounds, especially in Europe, where there is perhaps more of a problem with repression and over control, and who therefore prefer to emphasise the importance of understanding and expressing emotion (Greenhalgh 1994).

So Chapter 3 will explore the issue of emotional education in some detail, looking not only at more familiar work on emotional control but also at issues such as emotional understanding, self-expression and the enhancement of positive emotion, while Chapter 5 will look in more detail at how the taught curriculum can teach emotional competences.

Thinking clearly

There is consensus that a part of being mentally healthy is the ability to think clearly, to process information, to solve problems, to make good decisions, to set goals for ourselves, to defer gratification, to plan, and generally to have what that the HEA working party (1997) called a 'sense of reality'. Bremner, for example, sums up this competency as 'possessing and using the ability to integrate thinking, feeling and behaviour to achieve social tasks and outcomes' (1999: 1). Few of us would argue with these as useful and desirable competences, although, as we have suggested, we may differ as to their relative priority alongside other qualities, such as the ability to feel, to act or to express ourselves.

In line with the emphasis on emotional control and the management of feeling that we have noted has characterised work in this field, there is a massive amount of work which emphasises the importance of cognitive processing to mental health, and a good deal of effort has been put into teaching these competences to children and young people. Chapters 3 and 5 will explore the nature of these competences and examine work that has attempted to promote them in the school as a whole and in the classroom in particular.

The ability to grow

Those who work in child and adolescent development have usefully reminded us that mental health is not static, but is concerned with our ability to grow and mature psychologically, emotionally, intellectually and spiritually (Chwedorowicz 1992). Furthermore, what is mentally healthy depends on our age and stage, or as Winnicott, a major force in child development, put it: 'Health of the psyche ... is a matter of maturity' (1984: 55). Certain behaviour and attitudes may be appropriate at one stage and inappropriate at another, and we need to watch out for young people becoming 'stuck' in certain phases. Similarly, we need to recognise that change is healthy and normal, that, for example, we should expect a certain amount of resistance and rebellion from adolescents if they are successfully to negotiate their key task of finding their own identity. We also need to recognise that adults, such as teachers, are also at a particular age and stage, which may in itself give them issues to deal with in relating to young people: for example, teachers who feel their youth has slipped by may be tempted to vicariously identify with the young in ways that are not helpful for either party.

So this book will bear in mind the need for a developmental perspective for both young people and their teachers. Chapter 3, for example, looks at the changing needs of adolescents, while Chapter 5 looks at the importance of fitting the curriculum to the age and stage of pupils, and finding out where they are starting from.

Resilience

A key way in which we grow is through meeting challenges, or as the old adage says: 'what doesn't kill you makes you stronger'. Given that negative experiences are the stuff of life we cannot hope to avoid them, and so an important aspect of mental, emotional and social health is the ability to process difficult experiences, to learn from them and then move on, shaking off the negative feelings they can provoke rather than letting them fix us in the past, hold us back and drag us down. The HEA summarise mental health as 'the ability to use psychological distress as a development process' (1997: 15), while Jenkins, McCulloch and Parker give the process a rather biological spin with their definition of mental health as 'the ability of the mind to heal itself after shock or stress' (1998: 5).

Again, there is controversy on these matters. A psychotherapeutic approach would suggest that we should first explore a negative experience and the feelings it produces before we can move on from them, and that if we do not allow time for this the feelings will surface later. In contrast, cognitive and behaviourist approaches suggest that there is no physiological basis for this 'hydraulic' model of emotion, that dwelling on negativity simply fixes it in the mind, and that it is preferable simply to replace negative thoughts with positive ones and learn new behaviours. In practice a wide range of approaches has its uses, being appropriate at different times and for different degrees and types of problems. Therefore, this book will make use of work that emanates from a range of different traditions, while attempting to place it within a coherent framework.

The ability to make relationships with others

There is more or less total consensus both that the ability to make relationships is a central mental health competency and that warm personal relationships are an essential determinant of mental health. The HEA working group that attempted to define fundamental principles in this area (HEA 1997) made a lengthy list of the personal attributes that the group thought constituted mental health: they included the ability to form attachments; to bond; to connect with others; to make, maintain and break relationships; to manage conflict; to belong; to feel and show acceptance; to demonstrate good communication skills; to participate; to tolerate difference; to value others; and to feel a sense of mutual responsibility.

Our relationships with others are essential to any sense of well-being: the feeling of being loved and belonging is, as Maslow (1970) showed so clearly, one of our most basic needs, one on which many other needs, such as self-esteem and the ability to learn, are based. Relationships are not just what happens to us: from an early age we influence the behaviour of our carers to us. Recent work has demonstrated that the ability to relate to others is largely variable, but that it can very much be learned. It is vital that young people learn the competences that help them make and keep warm human relationships as they determine our level of success and fulfilment in virtually all aspects of our lives, not only our sense of mental well-being, but also our ability to learn effectively and to find and keep a job for example. Clearly too, if we argue that mental, emotional and social health depend on the creation of healthy environments, then we need to know what kind of relationships make the school environments more or less supportive.

Again, this area is by no means simple or uncontroversial. There is an issue about how far the promotion of mental, emotional and social health should be about encouraging people to accept, fit in and be socially compliant, and how far it should encourage people to be critical, autonomous and challenging, while encouraging others to accept and tolerate that difference. This issue is not often made explicit and, as a result, many programmes that teach social competences are unreflectively but strongly normative and based on a set of values and assumptions about what constitutes acceptable behaviour and attitudes that some groups, particularly those from outside of the mainstream, can find alien.

In recognition both of the importance of relationships and of some of the controversies within the area, Chapter 2 will suggest that warm, supportive relationships are one of the most fundamental principles of healthy and effective schools, but that schools need to be careful of being too normative, ensure that they allow for a reasonable amount of autonomy and diversity, and value cultural, social and ethnic diversity. Chapter 4 is largely concerned with how we can help pupils and teachers realise the social competences that help people achieve positive relationships, and which includes helping them achieve the autonomy to be different and critical if they wish.

Empowerment

A 'bottom up' approach

A key principle that needs to run through all health promotion activity, whether for communities or for individuals, is empowerment. Empowerment is widely vaunted as a key goal for health promotion (Tones and Tilford 1994; Hagquist and Starrin 1997). Empowerment is a concept that came originally from community development projects in the late 1970s and, as the name suggests, is essentially concerned with the distribution of power. It is about the active participation of all involved in a process, especially those who are intended to benefit from it, using what is often called a 'bottom up' rather than a 'top down' approach (Beattie 1991) in which the action or process is done with, rather than to, people.

The Ottawa Charter placed empowerment at the heart of health promotion when it defined the latter as 'the process of enabling people to increase control over, and to improve, their health' (WHO 1986). The Charter also suggests that health is 'a resource for everyday life, not the objective of living'. Thus, the goal of health promotion activity is not to produce some imposed state of perfect health, but to support people to be as healthy as they wish to be. The task of the professional working within an empowerment approach is not to direct people as to what they should do, or determine or plan the process for them, but to enable and facilitate people to help themselves achieve their own goals. The goals of empowerment are thus self-determination, independence and freedom – goals to which, as we shall see, social and affective education can make a major contribution.

The empowerment of individuals is not enough; on its own it can lead to aggression, rampant individualism, competition and social fragmentation. We also need a concept of social empowerment, aimed at groups and communities, which brings together self-empowered individuals and works with them to build a sense of mutual responsibility to build supportive communities, change personal and social circumstances, challenge political structures and create healthy environments (Freire 1973; Catford and Parish 1989).

Democracy

Strongly linked with the principle of empowerment, the principle of democracy has long been seen as central to health promotion in general and health promoting schools in particular (WHO 1997a). It is especially dear to those countries from northern Europe that have strong left-wing traditions: health promoters from Denmark have been particularly active in exploring ways in which schools can become more genuinely inclusive and participatory (Bruun Jensen 1994; 1997). Democracy has special resonance too for countries of eastern and central Europe that have been suddenly faced with the imperative to move their schools from being agents of a closed and repressive social structure to one that is open and liberating. Schools in these parts of Europe have naturally tended to be traditionally authoritarian in their ethos and didactic in their methodologies, and they are thus now especially concerned to explore ways in which they can rapidly shape themselves into more democratic and participatory organisations, pushing against the habits and attitudes of some fifty to eighty years of history (Parsons *et al.* 1997). Ironically, in western Europe many are increasingly alarmed at the extent to which young people have become alienated from the democratic process, and are engaging in a drive to promote citizenship education in schools and to foster greater political understanding and involvement at a national and at a local and community level.

So the principles and practice of the promotion of personal empowerment, social empowerment, and democracy will run through the whole of the book. Chapter 2 will suggest that the extent to which the whole school environment encourages participation and autonomy is demonstrably linked with greater school effectiveness. Chapter 5 will pick up these themes in relation to the taught curriculum, and Chapters 3 and 4 will concern themselves with the competences that individuals and groups need to acquire to become empowered, and how schools can best promote them.

Mental, emotional and social health should be capable of being evaluated

Evidence-based practice

As a vast field that makes use of a wide range of disciplines, contexts and agencies, health promotion is potentially boundless and therefore capable of being dismissed by those from the health services with whom it interfaces as vague and woolly. Conscious of this, many in health promotion have devoted a great deal of effort to considering how its effectiveness should and could be evaluated (Tones and Tilford 1994). Recently, health promotion has energetically followed the lead of medicine in its attempt to build a strong 'evidence base' for its work, a theme that is currently dominating much work and output in health promotion publishing (Davis and Macdonald 1998; Perkins *et al.* 1999).

Evaluation is now also a major fact of life in schools. The increase in emphasis on accountability and performance indicators means that schools and teachers are becoming used to, if not always happy with, the need to demonstrate their own effectiveness. There is also a strong tradition of research and evaluation in relation to specific work on interventions to promote emotional and social learning, especially in the US, which comes from the highly empirical world of experimental psychology where much effort has been put into reviews of social and emotional learning pro-grammes (CASEL 1998; Durlak 1995; Durlak and Wells 1997). So education as a whole, social and emotional education, and health promotion, all concur on the central importance of evaluation, and we need therefore to ensure that efforts to promote social and affective health are accompanied by valid and appropriate evaluation of their effectiveness.

Evaluation within the ENHPS

The ENHPS has always taken the issue of evaluation seriously: schools were only selected for the Network if they were prepared to facilitate evaluation and disseminate its results (McDonald and Ziglio 1994). There have been a few national evaluations, but the main thrust of international evaluation has been through the 'EVA' project at the Free University of Brussels (Piette 1995) which has developed both the theory and practice of evaluation in this area. It has more recently been complemented by work based at Christ Church University College, Canterbury (Parsons *et al.* 1997). The first conference on evaluating the ENHPS was held in Thun, Switzerland, in 1998 and its report will shortly be available from the WHO. So examples of practical experience are beginning to inform thinking in this area.

Health promotion is generally tough to evaluate (WHO 1998b), par-ticularly approaches that use a multi-variate 'settings' approach, so evaluating such a multifaceted concept as the health promoting school idea is naturally proving to be a major challenge (St Leger 1999). Evaluating such nebulous concepts as mental, emotional and social health promotion presents an even further stage of difficulty, so it is unsurprising that, in Europe at least, most evaluations of school-based health promotion have focused on physical health only. Now some of those involved in the promotion of social and affective health are calling for the creation of valid and reliable measures of social and affective well-being (NFER 1995; Stewart-Brown 1998). However, those who have tried to evolve such indicators have found the task very difficult, and concluded that measures and indicators will always have to be specific to a particular initiative in a specific context (HEA 1997).

Consensus is starting to emerge about the key principles of evaluating the health promoting school – principles that are capable of being applied to mental, emotional and social health (Pattenden 1998; WHO 1998b; Springett 1999). All agree that the evaluation process must first and foremost be congruent with the principles of health promotion. For example, if we are to respect the principles of holism and diversity, it is clear that it is best to collect a range of data from a wide range of sources, use a variety of tools within a portfolio approach, and draw on a variety of disciplines and approaches if our evaluations are to do justice to the complexity of the health promoting school idea (WHO 1998b). There needs to be a balance between rigour, the needs and perspectives of all the participants in the process, and the resources available (Springett 1999). If the evaluation is to be empowering, in others words participatory and bottom up, all stakeholders, such as teachers, parents, pupils and community members, need to be involved at every stage of the process, consulted about all aspects of it before it begins, involved in the data collection and interpretation and in the implementation of any outcome (Springett, ibid.). That way all parties are more likely to feel that they have ownership of the process, have learned something useful from it, and have the motivation to put the results into practice.

The uses and limitations of the experimental approach

There is a major controversy over the extent to which evaluations must contain an element of control. There has been a drive, driven initially by medicine, to undertake 'systematic reviews' of research studies and to guide busy health professionals through the wealth of conflicting evidence by providing summaries of best evidence. Health promotion has undertaken many such large-scale reviews, including some of mental health interventions (Hosman and Veltman 1994; Tilford *et al.* 1997). Although, in theory, the evidence considered for these reviews could come from many different types of study, in the highly medicalised world of evidence-based health care and systematic review, the touchstone has almost invariably been the randomised control trial (Jelinek 1991). Many of those who come to health promotion from the health service believe that only health promotion evaluations designed with a control group to compare with the group that received the intervention meet proper standards of scientific proof, objectivity and validity (Donaldson and Donaldson 1993).

However, many who come to health promotion from other backgrounds than the health service, for example, from education or social science, believe that the experimental approach has strong limitations when applied to health promotion in general, and even more so when applied to the evaluation of social and affective health (WHO 1998b). An empirical demonstration of this is provided by Chapman *et al.* (1999) who report that, when they included in their 'review of reviews' of school health promotion interventions only those studies that included some controlled element, they were left only with studies of limited classroom interventions on specific topics that related to health-related behaviours, for example, mostly drug abuse, exercise and nutrition. They could include no reviews of health promoting schools, other holistic approaches, broad school health promotion programmes, the promotion of wellness as opposed to prevention, or empowerment, even though they felt that these were the most important issues of all (Stewart-Brown 1998). Other earlier reviews have came to similar conclusions (Hosman and Veltman 1994; Tilford *et al.* 1997).

In recognition of this narrowing effect, the controlled, experimental approach is generally regarded as an inappropriate model to use when evaluating the kind of holistic, ongoing, processual and multifaceted interventions that the 'settings' approach gives rise to, such as the health promoting school (WHO 1998b; Springett 1999). The health promoting school approach is seen as containing too many confounding factors: it is essentially concerned with modifying the whole environment and thus the variables involved cannot be kept constant without missing the whole point of the process, or at least without being such a large-scale and expensive study as to be beyond the reach of most. Such an extensive and controlled study was carried out on the English ENHPS (HEA and NFER 1997a) and was indeed extremely expensive.

However, we do not need to dismiss the experimental approach entirely. It sets a standard for objectivity and the burden of proof that is a useful yardstick, not least in convincing sceptical outsiders and hard-nosed funding bodies. Although it cannot hope to evaluate a settings approach, it can help us look at some of its constituent parts, including specific efforts to promote mental, emotional and social health. The large database of projects held by the Collaborative for the Advancement of Social and Emotional Learning (CASEL) (CASEL 1998) contains reviews of over 700 studies of interventions on emotional and social health in schools, which aim, for example, to teach communication skills, social skills, counselling, assertiveness, self-esteem building and conflict resolution, and about a quarter of which manage to include elements of control. So the experimental approach has its uses in evaluating certain aspects of specific interventions to develop emotional and social competences as part of a wider repertoire and portfolio of strategies.

The use of evidence in this book

This book will be, as far as possible, 'evidence-based'. It will examine both the principles that surround the health promoting school idea and the extent to which there is yet the evidence to support them. It will, where possible, look for support for its assertions from controlled studies, but will by no means restrict its focus to them, recognising that a wide range of types of study can increase our knowledge of what works, that unevaluated initiatives can give valuable guidance, and that in any case we must not reduce our concerns to mindless empiricism. Principles and perspectives must frame our inquiry if it is to have a vision of what could be as well as what is, and these necessarily sometimes run ahead of the detailed evidence.

2 Creating a supportive whole school environment

Goals of this chapter

This chapter starts by outlining the evidence for using a whole school approach, and explores the principles that schools need to bear in mind when developing whole school programmes on mental, emotional and social health. It then draws on studies of school effectiveness to suggest that four factors are essential in ensuring that schools promote both academic and social learning and affective learning. It uses these factors as an educational framework within which to locate the principles of health promotion and to examine ways in which the features of the school environment, such as climate, ethos, management and relations with the outside world, can be made more supportive of mental, emotional and social health.

The principles of whole school programme organisation

A whole school approach

Chapter 1 outlined the eco-holistic settings approach, which is currently being developed in Europe and elsewhere through the health promoting school idea. Whole school approaches of various kinds have long been fairly common in the US school system, where they tend to use the terms 'comprehensive' or 'environmental' to describe approaches that go beyond the taught curriculum to work on wider aspects of the school environment (*Journal of School Health*, 1990; Cohen 1995; CASEL 1998). Such multidimensional strategies, which work on a range of interrelated and complementary fronts at once, have been shown to be much more likely to make long-term changes to pupils' attitudes and behaviour across a wide range of issues than are specific, limited, unidimensional programmes. For example, Durlak (1995), Durlak and Wells (1997) and the US Government General Accounting Office (1995) reviewed hundreds of different types of programmes designed to promote what the reviews termed 'prosocial' behaviour in schools, including reducing alcohol, tobacco and drug use, and violence. All three reviews concluded unequivocally that environmental programmes were much more effective than those that used curriculum projects alone.

The findings of these and other such studies have been remarkably consistent as to what are the most crucial features to include in a whole school approach. Vital features have proved to be: positive staff–pupil relationships; staff development and education; teamwork; the active involvement of parents, the local community and key local agencies; starting the approach early with the youngest children; and having a long-term commitment to the programme. The more effective programmes also use a broad and generic rather than a topic-based approach, focus on skills, attitudes and values rather than information and facts, are sensitive to the needs of pupils, especially those from different ethnic and social groups, and are developmentally sensitive to the age and stage of the pupils. Programmes also work best in schools with strong leadership and clear disciplinary policies. All of these are features that will be discussed further in this and later chapters.

We will now examine the general principles that schools need to bear in mind when developing whole school programmes.

A high profile and coherent approach

There is a strong consensus among those who have developed successful comprehensive approaches that mental, emotional and social health has to be high profile, not tucked in between other matters and topics that the school perceives as more important (Elias 1995; Elias *et al.* 1997). A proactive concern with this issue needs to come right from the top and permeate every aspect of school life and learning. The approach and strategy need to be explicit, with all involved, including teachers, pupils and parents, being made aware that promoting mental, emotional and social health is a key priority, and being clear about why and how they and the rest of the school are setting about it. Every teacher needs to believe that they and their subject have an active part to play in the total enterprise, whatever their specialism, and themselves receive education and support to make this a reality.

Such a holistic and integrated programme will not happen by chance: it needs to be planned and coordinated within a coherent framework (Elias *et al.* 1997), otherwise the school may fall into the trap of using a 'smorgasbord' approach, with individual teachers picking and choosing from different initiatives, projects and materials in a way that is confusing for pupils and which will almost certainly be replaced by the next fashionable issue that comes along. A coherent and coordinated approach is especially necessary for helping pupils with behavioural problems:

Walker (1995) looked at what schools can do to prevent antisocial behaviour, and concluded that schools needed a school-wide discipline plan to manage the classroom environment effectively, teach social skills explicitly, manage anti-social behaviour in the playground and, once again, involve parents and the community.

Experience in health promoting schools has shown that it is beneficial for each school to appoint a coordinator whose task it is to ensure synergy and harmony between the various parts and participants, and between the school and the outside community (WHO *et al.* 1993). Ideally, such coordinators are trained for the task, have time allocated to them to do it, are themselves fairly senior members of staff, and have the strong and active support of the head teacher and senior staff, perhaps through a steering committee. The role of coordinator is, given the holistic nature of the enterprise, a broad one. For example, in a school in New Jersey in the US the role of coordinator of social and emotional health included not only curriculum coordination, but also convening and chairing staff meetings on the issue, training new staff members, outreach work with parents and the community, and editing social development newspapers (Elias *et al.* 1997).

An approach which is right for the school

Schools that are developing new approaches are naturally keen to learn from the experience of those who have gone before them. Of course, existing programmes have a great deal to teach those starting out in the field, but it is rarely wise to try to import them lock, stock and barrel into a new setting. Social and affective education need to be tackled in a way that suits the nature and ethos of each individual school, and be adapted by individual teachers to fit their own style of working. Schools need to be particularly cautious in simply adopting approaches that have proved successful in other countries as they may well come from very different cultural and educational backgrounds and traditions: US programmes are, for example, often too pre-planned, top down and normative to be usable in a European context without careful adaptation. The exact nature of the approach must be up to the school to determine, and indeed Elias and his colleagues (Elias *et al.* 1997), who have a vast amount of experience in this field, claim that no project or initiative in this area has lasted that was not designed to fit within a particular school, and that those that are not are destined to sink after a short while. Pre-prepared initiatives have been shown to 'fade out' more quickly than those that are generated by the school itself (Moos 1991). Teachers are generally more motivated if they are involved in planning, design, evaluation and staff development than they are if they are working with initiatives that have been worked through elsewhere (Little 1982).

So, when planning a programme, the first step is for a school to find out where they are starting from and to build from there. Any new approach needs to fit within the school's existing aims, ethos, policies, rules, discipline and procedures, to work with staff strengths and teaching styles, and to meet the needs of the particular pupils and their community. Before making changes, it is worth reviewing such issues in order to decide on an approach that is suited to that particular school. As a result of such a review, schools will almost certainly find that they are already engaged in considerable work on social and affective education, perhaps without labelling it as such. Everyday work across the school, in interaction with pupils, in ensuring good order and discipline, in preventing bullying and violence, and in teaching mainstream academic subjects will certainly already involve teachers in tackling emotional and social issues. They will inevitably be, for example, liaising with parents, talking to pupils about their behaviour and feelings, managing classroom interaction, encouraging shy pupils, building confidence and self-esteem, and getting pupils to work cooperatively together.

A curriculum review will also almost certainly show that the school is already engaging in some kind of personal, social and health education activities that specifically support mental and emotional health: they might include lessons in life skills, citizenship, career education, family life education, sex education, AIDS education and drug education. The connections between these curriculum areas and more generic mental, emotional and social health are very much there to be made (as we shall attempt to show in Chapter 5). Bringing out the links between the school's everyday activities and existing teaching programmes and social and affective education can provide a valuable starting point in persuading teachers that this is an issue about which they already know a great deal, which can in itself be empowering and motivating for further action.

A long-term perspective

Programmes need to be given sufficient time and resources if they are to work, and schools need to take a long-term approach to work in this area and not expect too much too soon from any changes they institute (Elias *et al.* 1991). Children and young people have spent their whole lives learning patterns of behaviour and internalising their beliefs, and cannot change them overnight. Teachers, too, need time to learn new competences, to see the benefits of them for their practice, to start to adapt the approach to their own styles and gain a sense of ownership. There is evidence that programmes that aim at developing emotional and social competences are more effective the longer they are in place, and most take years really to establish (Hord *et al.* 1987; Arora 1994; Lantieri and Patti 1996).

We need to take a long-term perspective on the learners' development too. Programmes are most effective when they take a developmental approach, which starts teaching about health, including mental, emotional and social health, very early on in the child's school career (Mental Health Foundation 1999). Studies consistently demonstrate that children need to be taught the kind of competences that will help them, for example, to avoid drug misuse or violence, at a surprisingly early age. Many of the issues and problems are best tackled in primary school when children are most amenable to help (McGinnis 1990). There is overwhelming evidence that the ability to change negative behaviour decreases with age (Loeber 1990), and that signs of difficulty can be seen very early and are best tackled when they are still mild (Rutter *et al.* 1998).

Having started early, programmes need to carry on, with key learning being reinforced throughout the learner's school life, spiralling through the curriculum with increasing depth and complexity over time (Bruner 1966). The style and content of the teaching will change as the learner matures, so in deciding what approaches and materials to use, teachers need to make sure that thought has been put into targeting them at particular developmental periods. For example, younger children mainly need the competences to be demonstrated by their carers and communicated through metaphor and imagery (Greenhalgh 1994). In contrast, older pupils and adults are more able to reflect consciously on the processes, using more words and increasingly complex and abstract ideas and principles (Rogers 1996; Greenberg and Snell 1997). Education for teachers needs to follow the rather different principles of adult learning, for example, by recognising the considerable prior experience that they are bringing to the situation, linking with that, and ensuring that there is a convincing rationale for what is being proposed.

Teaching in this area should not be seen as a series of 'one-offs', or restricted to a particular group of learners, age group or particular time of year, all of which have been shown to have little long-term effect (Botvin and Dusenbury 1989; Boulton and Flemington 1996). Nor is it helpful for pupils to experience gaps in their learning (Elias 1995). Learning about emotional and social health needs to be experienced regularly and consistently across the whole of the pupil's school career. Without such a long-term, developmental perspective, large amounts of time and money can be wasted: the relative failure of the massive US drug-abuse prevention project, DARE, targeted at children in elementary schools, to make a long-term difference to the subsequent behaviour of the same children as adolescents has been attributed to, among other things, a lack of follow-up sessions to the programme in the secondary school context (Dukes, Ullman and Stein 1996; Clayton, Cattarello and Johnstone 1996). Similarly, teachers will need a great deal more than a one-day workshop if they are to internalise the learning of new principles and provide serious support for school-based programmes. Learning about mental, emotional and social health needs to be built into teacher education at all levels – from initial training through in-service and continuing education.

A safe and supportive physical environment

It is important that messages from the school's physical environment are congruent with the social and affective messages that staff are wanting to promote. The Elton Committee, which examined the causes and possible solutions to discipline problems in the UK, concluded that the physical environment had a major effect on pupil behaviour and on pupil and teacher morale (Elton 1989).

All of the policy documents that outline the principles of the health promoting school make mention of the central importance of the physical environment to health (Young and Williams 1989; WHO *et al.* 1993). Most of the focus to date has been on the importance of the environment for physical health and safety, through hygiene, lighting, ventilation, heating and hazard avoidance (McKenzie and Williams 1982), to which unfortunately now may have to be added a concern to make the school secure from violent intrusion (WHO 1998c).

More recently, attention has also been paid to the impact of the physical environment of the school on mental, emotional and social health (Wulf 1993). For example, several ENHPS schools have attempted to make their schools more attractive, ecologically sound and pupil-friendly while very much involving the pupils in the process of transformation. ENHPS schools in Poland, for example, have divided up their large spaces, used more colour, displays of pupils' work, art, plants and softer furnishing, and made classrooms and staff-rooms more personal and comfortable with quiet areas with rugs, soft chairs and books for browsing (WHO *et al.* 1993). Some health promoting schools have been attracted by the idea of becoming a 'green school' and used the space outside to make a garden or wildlife area, often tended by the pupils, sometimes with the help of parents to do the heavy work in the early stages (Harris 1991).

Work on the prevention of bullying has increased our understanding of how the physical environment amplifies or reduces this problem. Many schools have found that they contain unsafe areas, tucked away from adult eyes, where bullying and intimidation can take place (Tattum and Lane 1989). The toilets can be a 'black hole' in many schools, a haven for dirt and bullies. Some nervous pupils make strenuous and health-damaging efforts not to use them; few linger long enough to wash their hands. Schools need to ensure that there are no 'no-go' areas for adults, and that all parts of the school are frequently visited in a routine and unobtrusive way (Olweus 1995). It is worth organising the playground so that no parts of it are out of sight, and making sure that playground and lunch-time supervisors and teachers on duty take their task seriously so that pupils are as safe outside lessons as they are in them (Elton 1989). There need to be quiet areas available for more timid pupils to go at breaks and lunch-times, where adults are unobtrusively present, and where they can work, read, play games or chat. The journey to and from schools is also often a dangerous time for some pupils, with taunting and bullying taking place on school buses, on the roads around the schools and very often up to the school gates themselves. Parents, bus drivers, school crossing personnel and local shopkeepers all have a role to play in reducing the bullying that can happen around the school (WHO 1998c).

Four key features for an effective school: relationships, participation, autonomy and clarity

Key factors support both social/affective and academic learning

We have said that this book will link the principles of health promotion and the health promoting school with work from educational perspectives. There has been a good deal of educational research on school environments and climates that has much to tell us about what kind of school environments are most effective, not only in terms of academic learning, but in relation to mental, emotional and social health. The findings of a wide range of educational studies have been impressively consistent, whether they are related to pupils' academic performance, social behaviour or attitudes to school, or to teachers' professional performance or morale. They have demonstrated time and again that the assumption that there has necessarily to be a conflict between the traditional academic goals of the school and social and affective goals is incorrect, and that evidence from research on educational environments directly supports the principles of the health promoting school.

Four key elements have consistently been shown to be crucial to school effectiveness in both its academic and its affective and social dimensions. They are: supportive relationships; a high degree of participation by staff and pupils; the encouragement of autonomy in staff and pupils; and clarity about rules, boundaries and expectations. Each of these four elements demonstrably leads to better academic achievement, greater interest in learning, fewer drop-outs from school, better teaching and higher levels of social competence, improved morale and lower absenteeism in both staff and pupils (Fraser and Walberg 1991; Wubbels, Brekelmans and Hoodmayers 1991; Tunstall 1994; Thurlow 1995).

Although separately the four elements are important, they are even more effective when they operate together. In practice they tend to reinforce each other, and are far more powerful when used in combination: for example, teachers who feel supported are more likely to set clear goals for their pupils (Moos 1991). Many of the studies of the various factors have found it more helpful to cluster them and look at them in combination (Hawkins and Catalano 1992; Solomon *et al.* 1992), and some researchers have even suggested that we cannot understand any of these features in isolation (Marshall and Weinstein 1984). The essentially symbiotic nature of the school environment returns us to the need to take what health promoters have called an 'eco-holistic' approach.

In recognition of the need to bring together the frameworks and principles of health promotion with those of education, we will use these four key features to structure the rest of this chapter, which examines ways in which the main features of the school environment, such as climate, ethos, management, and relations with the outside world, can be made more supportive of mental, emotional and social health. As we shall see, this educational framework proves to be a remarkably comfortable one within which to discuss the principles of health promotion: the two are reassuringly compatible.

Relationships

The evidence for the importance of supportive relationships

Studies have consistently shown that the quality of relationships in a school is a key factor in producing high levels of staff and pupil morale and performance: caring, warm and supportive relationships are essential if pupils are to learn, and teachers are to teach, more effectively. For example, a review of twenty-four studies from across the world suggested that pupils learn more and have higher attainments, enjoy learning, are more motivated and attend better if their teachers are 'more understanding, helpful and friendly' (Wubbels, Brekelmans and Hoodmayers 1991: 156). A review of twelve sets of classroom research across four countries showed that better achievement on a variety of outcomes, both cognitive and affective, is associated with classrooms with 'higher levels of cohesiveness' and 'less social friction' (Haertel, Walberg and Haertel 1981: 34). An emotional attachment to school, teachers and friends has been shown to be vital for academic success (Battistich *et al.* 1997; Hawkins and Catalano 1992; Solomon *et al.* 1992). Conversely, schools that are unsupportive and have poor relationships have been shown to induce depression and absenteeism in staff and pupils (Moos 1991). Poor relationships between pupils and staff and between teachers and their colleagues is one of the most commonly cited causes of staff stress (Kyriacou 1996), while high levels of support, particularly from the head teacher have consistently been shown to reduce the likelihood of teacher burnout (Sarros and Sarros 1992).

Given the centrality of relationships both to the creation of supportive school environments and to the well-being of individuals, Chapter 4 will be devoted to looking at how good relationships can be fostered, taught and promoted. So, we will leave this issue for now, not because it is not important but because it is covered in such detail elsewhere.

Participation

Evidence for the importance of participation

One feature of school life that helps people feel valued and cared for, and feel more warmth and concern towards the school and people within it, is their level of engagement and participation in school processes. There is overwhelming evidence that the level of participation that the school and classroom encourages is another key factor in producing high levels of morale and performance in both teachers and pupils and in both academic, and social and emotional learning (Moos 1991). For example, a study by Bryk and Driscoll (1988) in the US found that pupils in more 'communal' schools, in terms of having shared values and a common agenda of activities, were more interested in school and had better achievements than those in less communal schools, and that throughout such communal schools disorder, absenteeism and school drop-out rates were lower. These results were echoed by Battistich *et al.* (1991) in a study of six elementary schools in the US, who found that pupils with what they termed a 'high sense of community' showed significantly greater academic motivation and performance, liking for school, empathy for others and conflict resolution skills. In the UK, the Elton Committee of Inquiry, commissioned by the government in the late 1980s to look at the improvement of discipline and the prevention of violence in schools, concluded that 'the most effective schools seem to be those that have created a positive atmosphere based on a sense of community and shared values' (Elton 1989: 13). Similar results have been shown when looking at the extent to which individual classrooms are more or less communal in ethos (Schaps, Lewis and Watson 1996). Fantuzzo *et al.* (1988) evaluated twenty-six studies that directly compared teacher-initiated and managed classroom interventions with pupil-initiated and managed interventions, and found that the pupil-led interventions tended to be demonstrably more effective in changing pupil behaviour.

A sense of participation has a benign influence on teachers too: teachers who work in schools that are more communal are more likely to be satisfied with their work, be seen by pupils as enjoying teaching, have high morale and be absent less often (Byrk and Driscoll, 1988). Rutter *et al.* (1979), in their study of British schools, found that schools that were more effective in terms of pupil learning outcomes were also more likely to consider teachers' views and represent them fairly, and involve teachers in policy formation. We have already cited the study in the US by Little (1982) which found that where staff were involved in designing and evaluating teaching materials and teaching them to each other, they were more motivated and committed than when they were teaching programmes that were given to them to teach. A recent UK report on how some schools that have been deemed to be 'failing' have been 'turned around' suggested that a key factor which induces success is the degree of active involvement of all staff, including support staff such as cleaners and caretakers, in the decision-making procedures of the school (Devlin 1998).

Participation is central to the health promoting school concept. It is, for example, essential to achieving empowerment and democracy, and relates very directly to ensuring both equity and better links with parents and the wider community. So, we shall explore ways in which schools can address the issue of participation in some detail.

Ensuring participation in schools

Encouraging participation in the school context can take many forms: they include consultation of staff and pupils; a democratic, 'bottom up' approach to decision-making; and open communication (Greene and Uroff 1991). The role of the head teacher in a more participative school is as leader of a team of staff rather than as the apex of a rigid hierarchy, a team that consults pupils and parents about the running of the school, is responsive to their needs and wants, and attempts to create a sense of common ownership of the school's processes, policies and decisions and a sense of openness (Hoy, Tarter and Kottkamp 1991). Pupils' conferences and councils, pupils' parliaments and parents' councils have all been suggested as ways in which participative intentions can become reality (WHO 1997a).

Active pupil involvement in the running and management of the school has always been a major priority for the ENHPS. Many examples of innovations that actively involve pupils in the running of the school can be found in a recent publication of case studies from ENHPS, summarised by the title 'pupils as active dialogue partners'. They include pupil-run class councils in a primary school in Poland, pupil involvement on a multi-agency steering group to decide sex education policy for a school in Wales, and a pupil-run project that has improved the physical environment to make it more 'pupil friendly' in a school in a deprived area in Belgium (WHO 1997b).

In the US, pupils often participate systematically in building good relationships in the school through schemes that give them direct responsibility for each other, such as peer mentoring systems, induction systems for new year groups, 'buddy systems' for new pupils or those with specific needs, cross age tutoring, and using mixed age groups, for example, for pastoral care, sports teams, and so on. Such approaches take advantage of the increased skills and maturity of older pupils and help give pupils a sense of responsibility while providing younger pupils with positive and credible role models (Elias *et al.* 1997).

Including special needs pupils

We said that the health promoting school is built on the principle of equity. This implies that schools need to examine how they distribute energy, time and resources so that all pupils have what they need to learn and grow, and so that the education they provide is for children from the whole of the community. Everyone needs to benefit from school; not only the academic achievers, but also slower children and those with special needs. Schools need to be genuinely socially inclusive, promoting diversity by valuing equally the worth of all pupils. The ethos is very much at odds with a traditional school spirit of competition, survival of the fittest and achievement of the few.

It is now generally accepted that, as far as possible, pupils with special needs, including disruptive pupils, should be accommodated in mainstream schools (Elton 1989; Ainscow 1998). Exclusion is seen as depressing and alienating those pupils who are excluded. It also deprives the pupils who remain of contact with the range of people contained by society at large, and deskills teachers who have no opportunity to learn how to manage the full range of cultures, behaviours, and cognitive and physical abilities. So we need to find alternatives to the alarmingly growing tendency for schools, including primary schools, to exclude special needs and difficult pupils (Hayden 1997).

There is a great deal of evidence that all kinds of special needs are associated with related social and emotional difficulties. A review by Kavale and Forness (1996) found that, across 152 studies, about 75 per cent of students with learning disabilities manifested social skill deficits that distinguish them from comparison samples. Such problems have also been found to be associated with physical disabilities, such as hearing problems (Greenberg and Kusche 1993). Special needs pupils tend, unsurprisingly, to have lower self-esteem and be more likely to be rejected by their peers, show lower motivation and higher level of frustration which they find harder to manage, and be more likely to be alienated from school (Gurney 1988). So there is a good deal of overlap between learning difficulties and emotional and social problems.

Fortunately, the kind of actions that a school needs to help those with special needs and behavioural problems is exactly the same as the kind of actions it needs to take in any case to promote the mental, emotional and social health of all pupils. McMillan (1992) in the US and Rutter *et al.* (1998) in the UK separately reviewed the copious literature on which interventions are the most effective in helping at-risk and behaviourally disturbed pupils. Both reviews came to the same conclusions, which are that effective interventions begin early, work on pupils' self-esteem, give them plenty of personal support, guidance and counselling, teach them social and life skills, involve peers and parents in the process, and create a positive school climate. The Elton committee (Elton 1989) commented that it would reduce disruption and violence in schools if all teachers were taught to be more competent in classroom management and pupil motivation.

Furthermore, the teaching of social and emotional competences has itself been shown to play an active part in making the inclusion of difficult children easier. For example, two projects that taught 'difficult' pupils the kind of skills they need to fit into classrooms more easily and control their own behaviour, while helping their classmates both tolerate their behaviour more easily and positively support their efforts to become part of the mainstream, were shown to be very effective in helping the difficult pupils stay in the classroom, and without detriment to the learning of other pupils (Rogers 1994; Epstein and Elias 1996). There is also a role for withdrawal units within mainstream schools to give greater help and support to young people with behavioural problems, not as long-term containment devices but as short-term and highly focused bridges, which tackle the problems pupils have in proactive and clear ways, back to the mainstream classrooms. Some schools are finding that difficult children and young people can benefit from being given additional help with supplementary classes, rather than withdrawing them from their normal classes on a full-time basis (Potel and Bowley 1998). Both withdrawal units and the mainstream classrooms to which pupils return need to use the same calm and clear strategies for managing classroom behaviour so that pupils experience consistent messages, expectations and boundaries (Elton 1989; Briggs, MacKay and Miller 1995).

Of course, problems can arise when there is not enough funding, education or support to help hard-pressed teachers manage challenging and challenged pupils (Fletcher-Campbell 1993). For a school to be inclusive it may well have to be given substantial resources to make proper provision for the particular needs of some pupils, such as the withdrawal units we have mentioned, special language classes for children from migrant communities, classroom assistants to give extra help to those with learning difficulties, or the creation of access for those who need to use a wheelchair. Measures to increase inclusion might actually save money, provided some mechanism is introduced to redistribute it where it is needed. It has been estimated that, in the UK, when the cost to all the affected agencies is taken into account, the total cost of exclusion in 1996 (£81m) was nearly three times higher than it would have cost to teach excluded children in mainstream schools (£34m) (New Policy Institute 1998).

Making schools more socially inclusive

We have said that the health promoting school is concerned with equity, and that all pupils need to participate equally in the life of the school and achieve the best they can from it.

However, for many children from particular social and ethnic groups this is just not happening. Underachievement and school failure have long been a concern of many, but little has changed since the early 1960s when the issue first reached major prominence, and these problems continue to be some of the important challenges that face education in most countries. The statistics of the association of social class and ethnic origin with educational achievement are very well-known. In the UK, children from social classes four and five, and from certain ethnic groups, most notably Afro-Caribbean backgrounds, consistently do worse on all educational measures, such as tests of attainment, examination results and entrance to higher education (Foster *et al.* 1996). There is also an alarming ethnic bias in school exclusions: recent data suggests that Afro-Caribbean children are four times as likely to be excluded as white children (Smith 1998).

School failure has long been known to produce a whole raft of educational, social and personal consequences. In the immediate school context it can result in alienation from school, disruption, bullying and violence (Hargreaves 1967). In the wider social context it can lead to large-scale unemployment and thus to poverty, social exclusion and the creation of an underclass. For the individual it can bring problems not only of material deprivation, but of self-esteem and its consequences, such as poor mental and physical health and greater difficulty in making relationships. In an attempt to try to crack this age-old problem there is now in the UK a major drive towards social inclusion and greater participation in higher education by all groups in society (Ball 1998), in which campaigns schools are clearly in the front line. So schools need to have a strategy for tackling inequalities.

Some of the causes of school failure are outside of the school's direct control, having their origins in the experience of poverty (Robinson 1967). Poverty can be depressing and limiting for pupils, for example those who come to school from a background of inadequate nutrition and poor housing, and suffer from the illnesses and growth problems that can result, who may be depressed and unwell, finding it harder to respond to educational opportunities. The experience of poverty may contribute to a climate of violence in the home or to a parent's problems, for example with alcohol or domestic violence, which are fairly certain to have an impact on the child, perhaps making it harder for them to concentrate at home, making them more fearful and withdrawn, or conversely more aggressive as a way of coping.

But simple poverty is by no means the only explanation for educational inequality: children from different social class or cultural backgrounds achieve differential educational outcomes over and above any influence that can be attributed to the level of income in the home. To explain this, it was fashionable at one time to look to the attitudes that children bring from their home background as the cause for such underachievement. In the 1960s and early 1970s much was made of the issue of apparent 'cultural deprivation' whereby working-class and other disadvantaged groups were thought to perpetuate the 'cycle of deprivation' through the attitudes and assumptions transmitted from generation to generation (Douglas 1964; Bernstein 1975). Attitudes such as 'external locus of control' (a fatalistic belief that the world is outside of your control) and 'short-term hedonism' (a desire for satisfaction in the here and now rather than deferment of reward for later) have been said to lead to a lack of interest in education and of a belief in the value of hard work and personal advancement, which perpetuate social inequalities. Although such theories are not so often heard today, some current researchers, especially those from the psychological backgrounds and from the US, continue to locate the problem of underachievement in individuals and their 'dysfunctional' cultural backgrounds.

In the 1970s the pendulum swung the other way, and it was for some time fashionable to dismiss these attitudes as entirely mythical and to look to the school as the cause of inequality through its differential treatment of pupils (Keddie 1973). More recently it has been realised that to be so dismissive of the influence of attitudes is naive, unhelpful to those who have problems, and risks shifting the entire blame from one party (the home) to another (the school). But this is not to return to 'blaming the victim'. It is now seen as more realistic to conclude, however, that some disadvantaged groups may have attitudes that do not help their ability to succeed academically, but that these are a product of the real circumstances in which they find themselves (Graham 1984; Davison *et al.* 1992). For example, manual and unskilled workers do in truth have much less control over their working conditions than do more skilled and professional people, and can be laid off at short notice. They are less likely to own their own homes, and thus have less control over their living conditions. In these circumstances, seeing your circumstances as outside of your control and having a short-term hedonistic view that 'jam today' is a surer bet than the 'jam tomorrow', which never actually comes, may be highly reasonable beliefs.

If indeed some of the beliefs that are central to educational achievement come easier to middle-class and to white pupils than to working-class and black pupils, this need not be an excuse for fatalism and buck passing, but can be a spur to positive action. Such pupils will need even more positive and concrete experiences of personal success and control if they are to believe that change is possible. This is all the more reason to make sure that school gives such pupils an experience of success, is a place where they feel comfortable, where the cultural referents are familiar, where the language patterns they bring from home are not viewed as substandard English, and where they do not feel they have to give up their culture and become middle-class to succeed academically. Rogers (1994) describes an Australian school programme that explicitly taught teachers not to be fatalistic and determinist, but to start where pupils are and build on their positive attributes.

In any case we cannot locate the entire cause of educational underachievement with pupils and parents. We know from the work that was
carried out in the 1960s and 1970s on the influence of the school that
schools are by no means neutral bystanders in the social mobility game,
they have a strong role in amplifying or reducing the differences that
pupils bring with them to the classroom, and this effect continues
unabated to this day (Elton 1989). Schools can unwittingly be contributing
to the problems of inequality through their own attitudes and practices,
including through overt or institutional racism (Troyna 1993; Blair and
Bourne 1998). For some time we have known that many teachers have
unhelpfully low expectations of children from lower-class backgrounds
and certain ethnic groups (Fuchs 1973; Coard 1971), which can result in
pupils being given very different images of their own abilities, and different
educational experiences and challenges (Young 1971). More recent data
about teachers' attitudes are very worrying: one in ten trainee teachers has
racist attitudes, according to a recent UK survey (Wilkins 1999) and, as we
have seen, the problem of the exclusion of black children from mainstream
schools in the UK is growing rather than decreasing (Smith 1998).

Teachers tend to be drawn from a narrow range of social and cultural
backgrounds, and may thus sometimes see, or even create, behavioural or
educational problems where none exist by judging pupils by inappropri-
ately narrow norms and values. For example, the exuberance of some
West Indian children might be hard for white teachers to relate to, and
they may see 'behavioural difficulties' that need punishment and exclusion,
where they might more usefully see difference which needs celebration and
perhaps some tactful channelling and containment (Gillborn 1990). The
loud and jocular behaviour of working-class boys, which many teachers
find disruptive, may well be behaviour that makes sense in other contexts,
such as the street, the housing estate, the club or the workplace (Willis
1977). The basic approach that the school uses to teaching and learning
and its assumptions about what counts as educational knowledge can
never be neutral or culture-free, and some have argued that the individualised and competitive approach taken by most schools reflects more
middle-class and white than working-class or black values and cultural
patterns (Young 1971). It may be that collective approaches to teaching
and learning, which emphasise cooperation and group values, would be
more congenial for working-class and black children, and may indeed have
something to teach middle-class white pupils about solidarity and social
responsibility.

We have dwelt for some time on the issue of educational underachievement and social exclusion as until we start to crack this problem at the
school level there is little realistic hope that schools will make progress on
achieving the goal we discuss next, which is the forging of links with
pupils' homes and the wider community. The vision of the school as
working in partnership with parents and the community is one that has, as

we shall see, proved to be the most difficult aspect of the health promoting school concept to realise in practice. It may however be the school–home–community links, which we discuss next, that will prove to be a key way in which inequality and underachievement can be reduced (Ball 1998).

Participation by those outside the school

The level of participation of parents and the community in any intervention is highly influential over its success: many large-scale studies and reviews of research on whole school health programmes, especially those that attempt to promote social and affective health, have shown that programmes are considerably more effective if they involve parents and the community (Durlak 1995; O'Donnell *et al.* 1995; US Government General Accounting Office 1995; Elias *et al.* 1997; Durlak and Wells 1997). It is helpful then that many schools are attempting to break down the barriers that have traditionally existed between themselves and the homes and communities that surround them (Cullingford 1985), and see the school as an integral part of both family and community life, with frequent two-way liaison and mutual participation.

The health promoting school idea is strongly supportive of this outward-looking philosophy, and all recent policy documents on the health promoting school idea strongly promote the importance of the participation of parents, and work in and with the surrounding community. Many national networks of ENHPS schools have placed particular emphasis on developing links between the school and parents and the community, including in countries as diverse as Ireland, England, Romania and Portugal (HEA 1995b; HEA and NFER 1997b; Parsons *et al.* 1997; WHO 1997b). The school is seen as having a strong social role in promoting citizenship and contributing to the efforts that various agencies are making to build sustainable and healthy communities that encourage healthy social change (WHO *et al.* 1993).

Involving families

In line with the new inclusiveness, schools are generally making far more effort to involve parents in the life of the school than has traditionally been the case. In many cases, such involvement is highly supportive of the social and affective well-being of the school. For example, initiatives that attempt to curb bullying and violence in schools invariably make the involvement of parents of bullies, victims and other children their first priority at every level of the intervention – from dealing with the immediate incident to seeking support for the wider school policies and actions that are trying to tackle the problem (Olweus 1995; Tattum and Lane 1989; Robinson and Maines 1997).

Specific programmes to develop emotional and social competences have been shown in a wide range of studies in countries throughout the world to work better where schools involve the pupils' homes and families in the process (Walberg 1984; Haynes and Comer 1996; Gettinger, Doll and Salmon 1994; Ronen 1994). Useful approaches include asking parents to help pupils with assignments and projects that look at the applicability of social and emotional learning in the home context, such as communication skills (Elias *et al.* 1997). More adventurously, some schools are inviting parents to work with staff and pupils on planning and management teams, and acting as liaison officers between the school and its surrounding community, while others are inviting parents to help with teaching and mentoring individual pupils or groups (Chapman *et al.* 1999). A recently established project in Oxford, England, is involving parents in whole school development programmes that aim to promote more 'nurturing' environments in the home and in the school, based on praise, clear boundaries and positive discipline (Family Links 1999).

One natural way in which parents can become more involved is through extending education to them. Some schools are integrating adults into the routine life of the school by allowing parents and other adults to study for missed qualifications with pupils in examination classes. This has proved to have a very beneficial effect on pupil and teacher behaviour (Devlin 1998). Educational interventions with pupils with behavioural and emotional problems have consistently emphasised the importance of involving families and the community, which often involves teaching the parents the competences their children need to acquire (Kamps and Tankersley 1996). Parents of children who are receiving specific help have been shown to benefit from receiving help themselves, both by developing the parent' own skills and ensuring that the messages home and school give to young people become more congruent. For example, a controlled trial of pupils with a history of behavioural problems in class found that those whose parents received counselling at the same time fared significantly better than those who were simply counselled themselves or received no help (Hayes, Cunningham and Robinson 1977). Similarly, boys who were taught a social skills programme maintained their new behaviour much better if their parents were trained and involved in the process through home–school notes (Middleton and Cartledge 1995). The effects can work both ways, and social skills training has been shown to have beneficial impacts on pupils' behaviour at home, for example, programmes of conflict resolution in school have often been shown to reduce friction at home (Gentry and Benenson 1992; Johnson *et al.* 1995).

Working with, and for, the community

We have said that the settings approach sees the healthy community as the key to effective health promotion for individuals, families and groups. If we mean by 'community' a setting that is large enough to be able to sustain and support a range of public health services and care for its members, but small enough for people to identify with and call their own, such communities may well need creating. In many cases where people are living in isolation, alienated from each other and the outside world, and without adequate supports, such genuine, supportive communities no longer exist. The school is one of the agencies that is often seen as having a role to play in regenerating and sustaining a sense of citizenship, community and public responsibility (Pollack 1991; Weissberg and Greenberg 1997).

As we have seen, democracy, citizenship and community involvement are central to the health promoting school idea (Young and Williams 1989; Commission of the European Communities 1990; WHO *et al.* 1993; WHO 1997a; WHO 1998a). The vision of the health promoting school outlined in the official documents is one in which the health promoting school concept is understood by all in the community, including those agencies that are directly concerned with the school, and embedded in their philosophy and practice. There is close congruence between the goals of the school and the local community, with the community being included in school plans and closely consulted about how both sides can achieve cooperative working relationships. Members of the whole social mix in the community participate in the life of the school, bringing the contribution of the various social, cultural and religious groups, the public services, businesses and the local media into school life. Community representatives are found on the school boards and committees that plan the various activities that relate to health promotion, and indeed all aspects of school life. The school receives support from local health and education authorities and local media, and is an integral part of a wide range of formal and informal local networks. Pupils spend a considerable part of their time outside the school, giving and receiving from the community.

Successful examples of such two-way involvement can be found, including community links that are specifically designed to foster social and emotional health (Chapman *et al.* 1999). Such programmes are fairly common in the US, for example: Giuliano (1994) describes a programme of violence prevention in a US school in which the whole school programme of conflict resolution is supported by an advisory board made up of student, community and school leaders, a programme that evaluations have shown to be highly effective. Examples are increasingly to be found in other countries too. A UK version of the US concept of Communities that Care has been set up in three cities, focusing on community initiatives aimed at preventing youth violence (Anderson 1998). In Trinidad and Tobago 'Servol' (Service Volunteered for All) has been set up as a grassroots community development organisation working with preschoolers and adolescents (Guttman 1994). In Europe, the ENHPS has been instrumental in catalysing several examples of such positive links between school, parent and the community. For example, in ENHPS schools in both Belgium and Northern Ireland, parents and the local community have become involved in a wide range of aspects of school life, while at a school in Denmark, pupils established a swimming pool, cycle tracks and a club for young people in the local community (WHO 1997b).

However, evaluations of the ENHPS have shown that some participating countries have not found it easy to forge greater links between schools and their communities, although all continue to see the principle as important and say they are determined to keep trying (Parsons *et al.* 1997). Wider evaluations of health promoting schools elsewhere in the world suggest that the forging of links with the community is probably the least developed aspect of the health promoting school idea (Nutbeam 1992; St Leger 1999). We have a long way to go before such a vision of the school at the heart of the community becomes commonplace in practice.

Linking with other agencies

There is a new emphasis in the UK on 'joined up' thinking (Peatfield 1998), evidenced, for example, in recent government initiatives such as Health Action Zones, Education Action Zones and the New Deal for Communities, in which disparate agencies are increasingly being urged to work together (Mental Health Foundation 1999). Schools are increasingly seen as having a key role in working with, and bringing together, various health-related local agencies that work with young people. This is particularly important in the case of mental and emotional health, where a wide range of agencies, such as the health services, counselling, psychology, psychiatry, social work and the police, are involved. Such agencies may be working directly with pupils in emotional difficulties or with behavioural problems, in which case it is essential that all concerned work together and speak with one voice if an already confused and distressed young person and his or her family are to be helped effectively. It is important that approaches used by any specialist provision for those with special needs, such as withdrawal units, or one-to-one work by therapists, counsellors and psychologists, are clearly integrated with any approaches being used across the whole school, for example disciplinary procedures, systems of pupil motivation and reward and, if they exist, programmes of social and emotional competence building. In this way, all parts of the school experience continue to reinforce each other, and pupils again experience consistent messages – a principle that is particularly vital for those who are already having difficulties.

Schools might also invite specialist agencies to become involved in their mainstream work, sharing their expertise with teachers, advising on school policies or curricula, or becoming directly involved in classroom work with whole classes. In the UK, the Hackney 'Well-being in Schools' project has developed such a multi-agency project, which is proving to be successful, to develop positive health in schools (Ajmal 1998).

Within the health promoting schools network such linkage between the school and outside agencies is again more of a vision than a reality. There are some positive examples of the development of such links (WHO 1997b), but it is undoubtedly a major area of weakness in most countries at present (St Leger 1999). There is strong evidence that the link between the school and the health services could be more effective if there was more of a partnership approach and more integration of the health services into the everyday life of the school (Cohen 1995; WHO 1996).

Autonomy

The importance of autonomy

Warm relationships and a participative environment can be manipulative rather than educational. If schools are to be genuinely empowering they also need to aim at producing independent, autonomous learners. Autonomous learners are able to make their own decisions, be self-directed and self-disciplined, responsible for their own behaviour and learning, and intelligently critical of what they have learned and what is going on in the world around them (Elias and Kress 1994). There is strong evidence that the pursuit of autonomy is fundamental both for academic and for emotional and social learning. Research has clearly demonstrated that pupils learn better and are happier at school if they are encouraged to think for themselves and to work as independently as their age, stage and personality allows, and that pupils learn more, have higher attainments, enjoy learning, are more motivated and attend better if their teachers allow high levels of pupil responsibility and freedom (Wubbels, Brekelmans and Hoodmayers 1991).

Autonomy is a relative, not an absolute, concept, and pupils respond best, including when learning about emotional, social and health-related issues, where the degree of freedom is suited to their age, stage and personality (Moos 1991). Younger, less mature and more introverted and anxious pupils need higher degrees of structure and organisation, but still benefit from being given as much autonomy as they can handle and by being gradually encouraged to work more independently. Older, more mature and more confident pupils can handle higher levels of individual choice and autonomy. All pupils need to be moved towards independence and autonomy, whatever their starting point. Indeed, learning to be autonomous is particularly important for those who come from homes where it is not so encouraged.

Autonomy is a key issue for teachers too. The degree to which teachers have control over their own work and have leeway to make their own decisions has been shown to be fundamental both to their mental and emotional health and to their professional performance (Moos 1991). Studies across a variety of occupations have shown that giving staff greater autonomy has a wide range of benefits, including decreased stress levels, lower absenteeism and higher morale (Shaw and Riskind 1983). A survey of 574 Australian secondary teachers (Tuettemann and Punch 1992) found that lower levels of stress were associated with higher levels of influence and autonomy. Higher levels of control even appear to be linked to health outcomes, such as lower levels of heart disease: a major study of English civil servants found that those further up the hierarchy who have greater control over their environment tend, contrary to common sense expectations, to have lower stress levels than those lower down, despite having a higher pressure of work (Marmot *et al.* 1997). Research with teachers in Hong Kong suggests that female, younger and more junior teachers have higher stress levels than their male, older and more senior counterparts (Hui and Chan 1996). Where staff lower down the hierarchy are allowed more leeway to make their own decisions, high demands, which in more autocratic workplaces lead to burnout, tend in more democratic environments to lead to higher levels of performance and less reported stress (Moos 1991). It may therefore be that one reason why there has been such a remarkable rise in staff stress levels in UK schools, as indicated for example by increased rates of absence from work, drop-out from teaching and reports of low morale (Dean 1995; Leech 1995), is the increased level of outside prescription, control and surveillance with which teachers are having to contend (McEwen and Thompson 1997).

Autonomy and theories of health education

Autonomy is not as simple a concept as it may well appear, and how best to promote it is a complex and contentious matter. Health education has put a good deal of thought into what autonomy means and how it can best be achieved, and the models and theories it has explored are both helpful in themselves and link directly with educational theories of teaching and learning, as we shall see.

Traditional school health education has been based on what is sometimes called the 'rational educational' model, the fundamental premise of which is that people are basically rational and their behaviour, including their health-related behaviour, is driven by logically derived principles (Williams 1984). This approach would say that people simply need factually correct information and then they will probably make a sensible decision: if they choose not to, that is entirely up to them (Baelz 1979). Autonomy is then simply defined as the right of the individual to be told the facts and then be left to make their own choice.

The rational education model has however proved in practice to be far too naive to be of much use in empowering people to achieve autonomy. It fails to recognise the pressures people are under, and the real and imagined constraints that prevent some people being free to make sensible decisions and healthy choices (Tones 1986). Case studies of health education interventions (Cleary *et al.* 1985) and large-scale reviews of health promotion initiatives (Liedekerken *et al.* 1990; Veen 1995) have shown unequivocally that most unhealthy behaviour does not spring from a knowledge deficit: most people, including most young people, know very well what is good for them and are still unable to respond to these healthy messages. Even the most motivated find healthy lifestyles hard to sustain (Miller and Rollnick 1991). Simply providing knowledge about health behaviour is of little help to people, who remain where they are, stuck with behaviour they may no longer want, with attitudes that are hampering their own development, and apparently with no one to blame but themselves.

In contrast to the rational educational approach, some educators and health promoters, especially in the US, have made considerable use of the behavioural approach. This approach sees people as essentially made up of learned impulses, habits and responses: their feelings, beliefs and motivations are products of these behaviours, not the other way round. The assumption is that to understand people is simply to observe their behaviour and the cues that trigger it and the consequences that follow: that this is as far as any analysis needs to go. The behavioural approach is very popular in health-related contexts: for those who come to health promotion from a medical perspective, the self-evident goal is that people change their behaviour in a 'healthier' direction. A great many initiatives that have attempted to teach social and affective competences use a behavioural approach, concentrating on the teaching of skills and routines, as examination of any database of such programmes (CASEL 1998; Hendren *et al.* 1994) will immediately show.

A behavioural, skills-based approach is often seen as completely incompatible with the achievement of autonomy, but it does not have to be so. Behavioural approaches are not necessarily coercive and manipulative; indeed, when used with adults, even strict behaviour modification approaches are almost always voluntaristic, and the most successful behaviour modification programmes are those that people devise for themselves, with or without the help of professionals, to get their behaviour under their own control and to help them reach their own goals (Watson and Tharp 1985). But, although behavioural approaches can also be used with young people in empowering ways as we shall see in Chapter 6, in practice they are usually used in schools in ways that are top down and normative, with the desired behavioural outcomes specified in advance by teachers rather than negotiated with pupils. When used in these teacher-centred ways they could not be said to promote autonomy.

The need to be cautious about the use of a behavioural approach is not just an ethical position, it has a basis in the evidence: although there have been few empirical studies that compare behavioural approaches with others in the teaching of social and affective competences, in those that there have been, the behavioural approach has often been found wanting (Morgan 1983). It would seem that the behavioural approach can be effective initially, but that, used on its own, it has few long-term benefits, being ineffective in helping children and young people internalise their learning and generalise from it (Maag 1990; Palardy 1992; 1995; Elias *et al.*, 1997). Without grounding in deeper attitudes and values, skills can be empty, shallow and easily changed. So we need to make use of the many useful insights that have been gained through using a behavioural approach but locate them within the broader perspective, empowerment.

Those who support an empowerment approach would say that if we really want to produce autonomous and reflective learners, we need to go beyond knowledge and behaviour, which are relatively superficial aspects of learning, and concern ourselves with their determinants, which are the attitudes and beliefs of individuals and the social context that shape them. Carl Rogers (1961), a highly influential educationist, characterised certain approaches, such as behavioural and rational educational approaches, as imposed learning or 'mind' learning, which 'takes place from the neck up', does not involve feelings or personal meanings, and has no relevance for the whole person. He contrasts it with 'significant' or 'experiential' learning, which is pervasive and meaningful and 'makes a difference in the behaviour, the attitudes, and perhaps even the personality of the learner' (Rogers 1983: 20). He has summarised mental growth as a process of 'becoming'.

Rogers' views are supported by the study of cognitive and humanistic psychology, which demonstrates the extent to which our world, especially our social world, is an active psychological construct rather than a pre-given collection of facts and 'real' objects. 'Reality' is to a large extent the interpretation we place on it in our own mind, what Kelly (1955) called our 'personal constructs' or sets of meanings that we all build through our experience. We learn through a constant interplay of self with the world, a negotiation between inner and outer reality. What someone makes of an event depends greatly on their previous experience (Ausubel *et al.* 1978). So we come to a new experience with a mind that is already pre-organised by our previous experience, and the same event will be perceived very differently by, and have quite different impacts on, the various people who experience it. From the very beginnings of our lives, possibly even from the moment of conception, our experiences increasingly differentiate us from each other.

It follows that, while paying due attention to behaviour, habits and skills, it is essential to look deeper and understand the meanings that people ascribe to them. This is particularly important when working with adults, who usually need clear and acceptable reasons why they should do something (Rogers 1996).

An active approach

Empowerment has a great deal to say about practical methods for helping people achieve autonomy. It builds on the behaviour change approach in recognising the importance of habits and skills, but it takes a more holistic approach to human motivation by acknowledging the importance of attitudes, feelings and beliefs as well as behaviour (Tones and Tilford 1994). It draws on the work of cognitive psychology, which has conceptualised and named a whole range of inner beliefs about the self in relation to the world, such as 'self efficacy' (Bandura 1977), 'health beliefs' (Becker 1984), 'locus of control' (Wallston and Wallston 1982) and 'learned helplessness/optimism' (Seligman 1975; 1991). Such beliefs, when negative, can cause people to feel passive, powerless, worthless, and thus do little or nothing to promote their own health. People can be fettered by their own unhelpful notions, restricted through a lack of skills, and disempowered by very real social circumstances they have not the strength, power, confidence or competence to tackle (Graham 1984).

In order to help individuals and groups tackle the real and imagined barriers to the growth of autonomy, the empowerment approach uses the proactive and energetic educational methods that draw to a large extent on the worlds of personal development (Nelson Jones 1993) and counselling (Geldard and Geldard 1997). These techniques are seen as aiding autonomy by tackling the inner and outer forces that block it. Activities can include helping people clarify their beliefs and values, examine and understand their emotions, value themselves, get greater control of their habits, and develop their communicative and assertiveness skills (Hopson and Scally 1981; Anderson 1988). Active, and often experiential, learning methods are favoured as powerful tools for personal and social change (Rogers 1983). Groups are often used as well as one-to-one approaches (Dwivedi 1988), including self-help groups, which can both support and challenge individuals. We will examine such active approaches in greater detail in the chapters that follow.

Clarity

Evidence for the importance of clarity

Alongside the pursuit of warm and supportive relationships, active participation and autonomous learners, we need also to introduce the harder edged value of clarity, the final key principle in the effective school. Clarity involves people experiencing structure and boundaries, knowing what is expected of them and what they can expect of others, understanding what their role is, and what the norms, values and rules of the organisation are. Without clarity, people cannot feel safe enough to participate, give each other warmth and support, or gradually develop a sense of autonomy: the world becomes frighteningly boundless and people retreat into defensiveness. The need for clarity in human relationships and organisations has been proven time and again by a great deal of research: basically people do not work well in climates with high levels of ambiguity and uncertainty. Studies of the social and emotional development of young children have shown how vital it is that the child be brought up by trustworthy and consistent carers (Winnicott 1984).

In the school context, several reviews of research studies have shown that pupils learn more, have higher attainments, enjoy learning, are more motivated and attend better if their teachers show clear leadership and are certain of what they are doing (Wubbels, Brekelmans and Hoodmayers 1991). Studies have demonstrated that pupils achieve better, both cognitively and affectively, in classrooms with higher levels of goal direction and less disorganisation (Haertel, Walberg and Haertel, 1981). Rutter *et al.* (1979) found that pupils did better in more structured schools in which they received more praise and positive rewards and where staff had high expectations of them. Similarly, a study of eight middle schools, which attempted to improve pupil behaviour, found that improving the clarity of school rules and consistency of rule enforcement was a significant factor in ensuring success (Gottfredson, Gottfredson and Hybl 1993).

Teachers, too, do better where goals are clear, being more highly motivated and effective in their job performance (Little 1982). Clear feedback about the quality of their performance to pupils and teachers, as long as it is supportive, is strongly associated with greater satisfaction and more effective performance (Moos 1991). The role of the head teacher in providing clear, active and dynamic leadership has proved to be particularly crucial, for example: it would appear to be among the factors that contribute most to 'turning failing schools around' (Devlin 1998).

Boundaries

It follows from the principle of clarity that, in a well-run school and classroom that aims to promote mental and emotional health, the proper management of boundaries is essential. These boundaries include, for example, having high standards and being clear about what is acceptable behaviour and what is not, having explicit and definable expectations and goals, providing a structure of good classroom organisation and giving unequivocal rewards for good performance. The setting of boundaries does not have to be aggressive or punitive: they can be set in a positive, non-confrontational and non-threatening way.

As Greenhalgh (1994) has pointed out, boundaries are especially important in helping people cope with the uncertain feelings generated by beginnings and endings – from the micro level of lesson transitions to the more macro transitions of starting new terms, working with new teachers, starting new schools or leaving school. These times can be especially difficult for vulnerable children (Maciver 1998), bringing up feelings of uncertainty, abandonment and loss. Schools do well to pay particular attention to the need for rituals and routines that mark, ease and sometimes celebrate transitions. Procedures, such as preparing for the ending, allowing time to reflect on what has happened and what can be carried forward, and reminders that the group will meet again (if it will) can all help to ease these transitions so that the ending can be a positive sense of closure, rather than spoiling memories of what went before.

It is essential that teachers are themselves consistent, reliable and fair, which in turn demands that they are able to be themselves stable, calm and consistent. Only thus are they able to be good role models for their pupils in managing their emotions, and able to give the child the sense of stability and trust from which it is safe to explore and take risks. Teachers need to be clear about the boundaries that necessarily exist between themselves and their pupils, and not be tempted to cross or blur them to meet their own unmet needs. Pupils feel safer and more secure if their teachers are not trying to relive their own childhood or adolescence through vicarious identification with their pupils, and are more likely to respect teachers who are clear about the need for a proper and professional distance between them.

Positive expectations and climates

We have known for some time how significant teacher expectations are as an influence on the behaviour and attainment of pupils. Teachers communicate their expectations to young people not only in direct and straightforward ways, but also in indirect and less obvious ways, such as by verbally making subtle comparisons between pupils, by the number of times they make verbal contact with individual pupils and by praising or ignoring responses from them. Teachers themselves may be unaware that they are doing this. In a classic study, Rosenthal and Jacobson (1968) demonstrated that pupils whom teachers were told were more intelligent did better over time than their counterparts, even though there was originally no difference between them. Reviewing the literature ten years later, Hamacheck (1978) concluded that there was a wealth of evidence for the impact of teacher expectations on pupil performance, and the evidence for this effect has increased since. We have already looked at the impact on school achievement of the differential expectations that some teachers can have of working-class and ethnic children. It is important that teachers have positive expectations of all their pupils, and that pupils in turn have an optimistic view of what they are capable of achieving.

We have already noted that the Elton committee, which made recommendations on discipline and the prevention of violence and bullying in schools, suggested that it was vital that schools foster a positive climate (Elton 1989). One very useful insight of the behavioural approach is that people respond better to positive rewards than to punishment, and that it is more effective to simply ignore unwanted behaviour than to punish it, as punishment actually serves to fix behaviour by making it memorable (Bandura 1977; Nelson 1987). So it is especially important when dealing with difficult pupils that teachers focus on the positive, on what the pupil can do rather than what they cannot do, catch them doing something good and reward it rather than always being on the lookout for bad behaviour (Rutter *et al.* 1998).

Policies

A further way in which a school can achieve clarity is by producing explicit policies for action. In recent years British schools have been inundated with demands that they develop whole school policies on a huge range of issues, which range from traditionally controversial areas, such as discipline and sex education, to areas about which, in the past, schools have not needed to be explicit, such as literacy and numeracy. Some schools have understandably resented the imposition of these require-ments, and some may well have responded by drawing up paper policies, written by the head teacher alone, that do not relate to action in the real world. However, many schools have found the exercise of becoming clearer about their practice and arriving at a consensus on forms of action has been, in part at least, a beneficial participatory exercise. So school policies on issues that relate to mental and emotional health, such as discipline, bullying, racism and home–school relationships will have an important part to play in shaping the overall context (Elton 1989). However, as St Leger (1999) points out, there is not yet sufficient evaluation of this aspect of the health promoting school to be able to prove this conclusively, and few health promoting schools seem yet to see the development of policy as a priority.

Conclusion

This chapter has looked at a range of aspects of the school environment that can create the conditions for the promotion of the positive mental, emotional and social health of teachers and pupils, and link the school with its wider community. The principles and structures outlined in this chapter should also be seen as underlying the later chapters, which will explore more specific ways in which schools can help pupils and teachers develop the competences that are needed for social and affective health.

3 Developing self-esteem and emotional competency

Goals of the next two chapters

This chapter will focus on the competences involved in what Gardner (1993a) referred to as 'intra-personal intelligence', which is the ability to understand oneself, to form an accurate model of oneself, and to use this model to operate effectively in life. The following chapter will focus on inter-personal, or social intelligence. In practice, the two types of intelligence are often inseparable, so the distinction should not be taken too seriously, and these introductory remarks are intended to serve for both chapters. These two chapters between them outline some of the key competences that people need if they are to be mentally, emotionally and socially healthy themselves, and to be of help to others in developing social and affective health. Building on the principles and suggestions of the last chapter, they make some broad proposals as to how these competences can be realised in a school context.

There is not the space here to look in detail at specific ways in which pupils with particular acute or chronic mental health problems, such as clinical depression, suicidal tendencies, post-traumatic stress or eating disorders, can be helped. However, this book has drawn on the findings of the kind of work that has been carried out in helping people in severe difficulties, and the principles and strategies outlined here provide a general framework in this area. A school which adopted such principles and strategies should find that they very much assist with preventing mental and emotional health problems, detecting them, and helping pupils and teachers deal with them. As well as the references we will cite on specific mental health problems in the course of the chapter, there is a list of agencies that deal with mental health and schools, including those that deal with particular health problems, at the end of the book, which provides contact addresses for those who need more guidance.

The competences

We use the term 'competency' rather than the more usually employed term 'skills' because competency includes attitudes and knowledge, as well as skills. As we discussed in Chapter 2, if we wish to help people to be empowered and autonomous, we need to teach more than behaviours and skills: we need to help people think for themselves and develop sound and lasting attitudes and values, which direct their behaviour in consistent, fundamental and ethically sound ways.

The competences have been drawn from a variety of different disciplines – from school-based work on social and emotional learning, but also, and more unusually, from counselling, therapy, personal development and community-based work – areas that have not so often been applied in a school context. The competences are to be found within a vast number of texts and programmes, for children, young people and adults, which name, prioritise, order and combine them in different ways (for example, Goleman 1996; Elias *et al.* 1997; Salovey and Sluyter 1997). Although originally formulated in, and perhaps thus most relevant to, the US and Europe, they have also been shown to have some applicability across a wide range of other cultures (Eitan, Amir and Rich 1992; Guttman 1994; Lee 1994; Hon and Watkins 1995). The chapters attempt to get behind the specialist terminology of the various disciplines and programmes to present the competences in their most basic and generic form, and to link them with work on child, adolescent and adult development.

It is not suggested that these competences in themselves simply constitute a curriculum, nor should it be deduced that they could or should always be taught in a generic form. Children, young people and some adults find it very difficult to move between the general and the specific. The basic competences should be seen as 'building blocks' that need to be elaborated and made specific time and again, and combined in new ways and applied to new issues, topics, situations and subject matter. They are, in their generic form, as relevant to 50 as to 5 year olds, and so the chapters will often employ the term 'learners' to remind us of the relevance of these competences for teachers as well as pupils.

Building an accurate self concept and acquiring self-esteem

The idea of a self concept

The most basic task for our mental, emotional and social health, which begins in infancy and continues until we die, is the construction of our sense of self (Wylie 1961). Our development can be seen as centrally concerned with defining the self and the outside world in relation to one another. It is a dynamic, fluid process which takes different forms at different times of our lives. According to Rogers (1961), it is central to all other forms of learning: people will only learn if they feel that the learning helps to construct or maintain their sense of self, and will reject or block learning that is perceived as threatening to themselves.

To have a concept of self we need a concept of 'other' for it to contrast with. Very young babies do not have such a concept, and see themselves as the entire world. During the first and second years of life, a child learns to discriminate the 'me' from the 'not me' and, through touch, smell and sight, learns to recognise the boundaries between him/herself and the outside world. Gradually the infant learns that objects and people have a separate reality from him/herself, that they continue to exist even when they are out of sight, and that they can remain essentially the same even though their appearance changes (Piaget and Inhelder 1958). The dynamic relationship between self and other runs through all our development. For example, in some sense other people are 'objects' to all of us throughout our lives, and only partially real, although acquiring greater empathy can helps us to reduce the gap. In some ways, too, we sometimes objectify ourselves, or at least the parts of ourselves that we do not like or want to accept, by projecting them onto other people and experiencing them vicariously (Klein 1946).

Self-esteem

The self concept is made up of thousands of beliefs that we have about ourselves, formed largely through our interaction with others, and particularly those 'significant others' to whom we relate most often and most deeply, initially our parents or other carers, later our teachers and our peers. The resultant self concept is not neutral. It is highly coloured emotionally, and can be positive or negative, more usually it is a mixture of the two. A sense of positive self-esteem is generally seen as the essential for mental, emotional and social health (Macdonald 1994), and so much effort has been devoted to the study of its determinants. Coopersmith (1967) carried out ground-breaking and comprehensive work in this area, and suggested that the antecedents of self-esteem are the extent to which we feel valued by others, experience success in achieving our own aspirations, and feel significant and competent. A sense of self-esteem then helps us acquire defences against threat and anxiety.

Sadly, by no means all young people have a strong sense of self-esteem. In the survey by Gordon and Grant (1997), when asked how they felt today, one in ten young people said he or she felt 'useless' and/or 'a failure'. Teachers also often suffer from low self-esteem, which has been shown to correlate with their feeling mentally unhealthy, and having a lower commitment to teaching, more negative attitudes to school and higher stress levels (Lin and Lin 1996).

Helping children to acquire self-esteem

In Chapter 2 we looked at the importance of warm and supportive relationships and clarity in the health promoting school. It is indeed generally agreed that, from infancy onwards, a sense of safety and a sense of trust in the world and in other people is one of the most essential building blocks for self-esteem (Erikson 1977). As Bowlby's (1980) work on attachment demonstrated so vividly, children thrive when they have people in whom they can trust and on whom it is safe to be dependent, who provide a consistent, warm and approving foundation from which it is safe to venture into the world, secure in the knowledge that they can return at any time for positive affirmation that all is well and that they are doing the right thing. Paradoxically, it is only from the basis of such safe dependence that the child will feel able to move towards real personal independence and autonomy. The child's sense of security and consistency comes from feeling essentially loved unconditionally whatever they do, of experiencing him/herself as continuing to be loved and approved of, even when their immediate behaviour is not so lovable or easy to approve. If children experience such positive relationships and unconditional love, they come to see themselves through the eyes of their carers, including teachers, as having a good proportion of positive attributes, and will thus build a positive self-image.

Often, however, children do not experience a sense of being loved warmly and unconditionally by adults who can be trusted to be consistent: much can go wrong. Their carers may simply be indifferent to them, or inconsistent, affectionate one day and withdrawn the next, or be so needy themselves that they overreact to the child's negative expressions of emotion by withdrawing love or becoming hostile themselves. At worst, the adult may be a source of serious psychological or physical abuse and threat.

The child who cannot trust his or her carers has, according to Bowlby, two choices. One is 'anxious resistant attachment', becoming clingy and more dependent, ever looking for signs that they are loved and wanted. Such children with their attention-seeking behaviour are familiar to every teacher, which can be very wearing. Alternatively, the child resorts to 'anxious avoidant attachment', giving up on the hope of outer security and becoming prematurely self-reliant, but in a mistrustful and suspicious way, rejecting all forms of dependency as dangerous, expecting only the worst out of life. Such a defensive reaction has been commonly described in the psychological literature: Klein (1946) describes such a sense of self as 'paranoid–schizoid', Winnicott (1964) described it as 'false', Greenhalgh (1994), following Freud, calls it 'narcissistic'. Such a child sees him/herself as the only possible source of security, and believes that they have to be in control of everything, to have everything their own way or else nothing good will happen. Paradoxically, such children are easily tipped over from feeling omnipotent to feeling completely worthless if things do not go their way and they are not able to protect themselves. They tend to be unable to accept the negative sides of their nature, and have to project their own bad feelings onto others, who are seen as causing their rage or anxiety: they have no interest in or understanding of their own inner lives. Such children often set up the conditions under which the worst happens through their own difficult, antisocial and self-contained behaviour, thus confirming their negative beliefs. Such falsely confident and highly defended children will be recognisable to most teachers, and are likely to cause their teachers and classmates enormous problems with their need for control, their rages if they cannot have things their own way, and their inability to examine and own their own feelings and thus start to control them. They can test to the limit the teacher's ability to 'contain' their emotional outbursts and provide a stable, trustworthy context.

Self-esteem is vital, but it has to be realistic. Children who have not experienced the necessary boundaries can turn into 'spoilt brats', seeing themselves as the centre of the universe, all powerful beings, and other people as put on earth just to respond to their demands. Children who have not been encouraged to acknowledge their own negative emotions can see themselves as all good, and perceive their own difficulties and negative emotions as arising from others rather than from themselves (Greenhalgh 1994). So to have a healthy sense of self-esteem is not the same as believing that we are all powerful or all good: our self concept needs to constitute an accurate assessment of ourselves in relation to others if it is to help us operate effectively in the world. Rather than just thinking about helping children and young people acquire self-esteem, schools need to aim at helping them gain a realistic sense of who they are, their weaknesses and strengths.

Self concept and self-esteem in adolescence

The period of adolescence poses challenges for young people, and often even more challenges for their teachers and parents. For adolescents to reach maturity successfully they must complete what Erikson (1968) suggested was their key task, which is forming a separate identity, cutting loose from their background and becoming an independent adult. Adolescence is about finding your own way through, balancing the needs of the outside world with your own needs, finding out how to develop and establish dignity and self-worth, and distinguishing yourselves from others. This process of self-definition does not have to be experienced as traumatic by the adolescents themselves or by the adults who care for them, and the extent to which adolescence is invariably a period of stress and turmoil has been exaggerated. But the process is inevitably marked by a significant difference in the relationship between the young person and the adults who surround him/her, which adults can sometimes find threatening. Some work on adolescence has tended to view this stage as troublesome, difficult and problematic when it may be better viewed as the transient side effects of healthy maturation. Schools need to take a positive and constructive view of the changes young people are going through.

The changes of adolescence are partly due to hormone changes and the influence of intense physical change: adolescence is a time of high emotion, with feelings fluctuating wildly from day to day. Adolescents can become confused and distressed by experiencing so many conflicting and differing feelings, thoughts and sensations. The changes are also partly based on cognitive maturation: adolescents become capable of reflection, thinking abstractly, going from the specific to the general and are thus more able to see a range of possibilities and potential forms of action, and become able to stand outside of themselves and reflect on themselves, their strengths and weaknesses. They stop taking it for granted that things are right because an adult says so, and instead start to think for themselves and question what they are told. They often become very idealistic, forming a concern for the environment or animal welfare for example, and as they see the defects in society, start to blame the older generation for mistakes. Rather than seeing these challenges to authority as problematic, all of these new abilities and attitudes can be capitalised on when helping adolescents learn more about such issues as decision-making, self-control and self-motivation.

The peer group is often seen as a pernicious influence over young people's health, but it is inevitable that teenagers will transfer their need for 'love and belonging' to their friends and away from their parents and teachers, and place an emphasis on fitting in with codes of behaviour and appearance approved by the peer group, often to an extent that adults find incomprehensible. As they mature further, teenagers consolidate their personal identity and can become more separate from the herd, often forming smaller sub-groups within it. So there is no point in trying to fight the peer group: schools need to use its influence positively, and we shall examine the powerful ways in which peer education can be used when we look at teaching and learning in the final chapter.

It is important to recognise that young people will inevitably have different priorities to adults (Withers 1995). The more 'adult' values of settled, safe living, emotional stability and looking to the future may be quite inappropriate for those who have still to work out their own identity, for whom the 'play' of having fun and taking risks are a necessary part of healthy growth. The search for identity inevitably involves experimentation of many kinds, for example, with behaviour, appearance, friends, and often with drugs and sexual behaviour. Some of these manifestations can be very alarming for adults, and can indeed sometimes endanger the health of young people. While obviously taking proper care of young people, adults, including teachers, must not create problems where none exist, or overreact when a more low-key approach might allow a problem to resolve itself quietly. Adults also need to be able to recognise when development is not normal, when a young person is 'stuck' at a certain stage and needs to be helped to move on. They may need to recognise that sometimes the young people that older people find easier and more pleasant may not in fact be the best adjusted: an over-dependent teenager may seem easy to deal with, but may not be developing as he/she should.

Having suggested that adults must not see adolescents as necessarily problematic, neither should they abdicate their responsibilities. Adults have a very important role in providing the kind of clarity and boundaries that are so important for a feeling of safety, even if the young person needs to kick against it at the time. Adolescents need adults to lead their own lives, and are wary of their vicarious involvement. However, they need adults more than they care to admit, tending to notice what adults do and emulate it, but often not say so. The key role of the adult is to create environments in which young people can grow and feel good about themselves without too much obvious surveillance or over involvement.

Schools and self-esteem

One of the most important environments for influencing self-esteem, in young people and in children, is the school. Gordon and Grant's survey (1997) showed clearly that school is extremely important to self-esteem: about one-third of adolescents cited 'doing well at school' as the thing that made them 'feel good about myself' and it was the largest single influence mentioned. So schools need to do everything in their power to help all their pupils succeed, to encourage them to believe in themselves and their abilities, and to allow them to feel effective, successful and competent (Borba 1989). This may be tough for some schools that base their motivational strategy on the belief in the power of failure as a goad to action: it is likely that the persistent experience of failure that so many of our children undergo simply confirms in them the belief in their own uselessness. It is alarming that studies show clearly that young people become much more disaffected from school as they get older, with a recent major UK survey showing that nearly half of year-eleven pupils said they did not like school (HEA 1999). As we saw in Chapter 2, such alienation is much more likely to be found in particular social groups, most notably working-class and black pupils.

We suggested in Chapter 2 that warm and supportive relationships were an essential factor in school effectiveness in general and promoting mental, emotional and social health in particular, and that schools need to create positive climates. The type of school ethos that is most appropriate for the development of mental and emotional health is one in which the school is a place where each person feels safe, cared for and valued, which believes in them, which positively facilitates their growth, which listens to them, and which empowers them to 'be all they can be' (Wetton and Cansell 1993; Schaps et al. 1996). We need to ensure that all pupils feel respected and liked, and achieve some sort of success. The resultant high levels of self-esteem can partly 'inoculate' pupils against later threats to their self-regard, including those that come from the peer group. Pupils can be helped to realise that they cannot please all of the people all of the time, and empowered to 'bounce back' after disappointments. They can learn that it is possible to be true to their own values no matter what pressure they may be under. This is the foundation for personal autonomy, free choice and responsible behaviour. If young people feel valued by their teachers and their classmates, they will more readily accept ways in which realistic improvements to their work and achievements can be made, and this in turn encourages them to be more open and accurate in their own self-evaluations.

Emotional competences

'Emotional intelligence' and 'emotional literacy'

Having examined the importance of self concept and self-esteem, we come now to the competences that can help us understand and accept ourselves, and build a positive sense of who we are and who we might become. The basis for a realistic self concept is knowing ourselves, including our emotions (Greenberg and Snell 1997; Saarni 1997). To be well-integrated people, content in ourselves, able to build fulfilling relationships, and help others with their problems, we all need an ongoing, introspective awareness of our own inner emotional states, and to be aware of what we really feel. This is the most basic action competence of all, and few of us ever really quite master it. Recent work on the development of what Gardner (1993a) has called 'intra-personal intelligence' has made it clear that the ability to form an accurate model of oneself and the ability to use it to operate effectively in life are not just given, they can be learned, and schools can do a good deal to help young people develop them.

An important part of 'intra-personal intelligence' is the ability to understand our own emotions. Mayer and Salovey used the term 'emotional intelligence', which they defined as 'the ability to perceive accurately, appraise and express emotion; the ability to access and/or generate feelings which facilitate thought; the ability to understand emotion and emotional knowledge; the ability to regulate emotions to promote emotional and intellectual growth' (Mayer and Salovey 1997: 10). Emotional education is becoming fashionable, and several pressure groups, in the UK and elsewhere, are calling for schools to do more to address the issue of emotion in schools, often under the banner of the increasingly popular concept of 'emotional literacy' (Growald 1998; McCarthy 1998; Antidote 1998), a term generally first credited to Steiner (1984; 1999).

Gaining the ability to understand our own emotions and using it to shape our own actions are competences that are not only essential for our mental and emotional health; according to Goleman (1996), they are meta-abilities that are highly linked to academic and career success. He claims these abilities are far more predictive of later success than are IQ scores or scores in tests of traditional subjects. So it is a competence that schools would do well to foster in all their pupils and in their staff.

Bodily awareness

Bodily awareness is a highly useful starting point for getting in touch with the emotions, but one that is not often connected with social and affective learning in schools which is very often all based 'in the head'. As the earliest pioneers who studied the psychology of the emotions immediately realised (James 1890), the emotions invariably have an effect on the body. For example, anger leads to an increased heart rate, a clenching of the muscles and a feeling of heat in the face, and joy leads to feelings of physical lightness and energy. We need to learn to be sensitive to the effects of the emotions on the sensations of our own body, to what causes them, and our own reactions to them, monitoring them as they actually happen. However, evolving such awareness of the effect of the emotions on the body can be difficult. Even quite young children may have spent so much time denying their feelings that they are out of touch with their physical body and what it is trying to tell them: they may need permission and sensitivity training to perceive these sensations clearly again. The problem is likely to be more acute when we are working with older people (Damasio 1994).

Bodily signals can become confused and mistaken: for example, it is common to interpret the feelings of inner emptiness that negative feelings such as sadness or anxiety can cause for hunger, and to eat in a misguided attempt to feel better (Leon 1993). In any case, how we feel is sometimes by no means obvious, even to ourselves. Psychoanalytical theory has made a major contribution to the problem of self-understanding by recognising that many of our most significant feelings do not make it to the level of the conscious, but stay buried in our subconscious, manifesting themselves in other, more indirect ways. Psychoanalysis has evolved the labels of repression, denial and projection to describe what we do with feelings that we find hard to acknowledge, or which other people have told us are not acceptable to demonstrate. The body often becomes involved in this process, holding or manifesting our emotions in often surprising ways: a branch of psychotherapy, 'body psychotherapy', specialises in working on the holistic relationship between mind and body, and recognises that it is a complex, and often indirect and confusing, relationship (McNeely 1987; Juhan 1987).

While not advocating that teachers dabble in amateur psychotherapy, it is important to recognise that acquiring inner awareness is not an easy or a superficial ability: learners need time to get in touch with their feelings, reflect, be introspective and develop their sensitivity. They may need to gain insight from others who can reflect back to them how they seem to the outside world, for example, what their tone, body language or actions seem to be saying, which may be in contradiction to what they consciously intend (Nelson Jones 1993). They may benefit from taking part in physical activities that help bypass the conscious mind and express inner feelings more directly, such as dance or painting, and perhaps be helped to talk about and reflect on the process. Young children will benefit from being encouraged to experience the physical world firsthand through their five senses, including touch, smell and taste, as well as the more familiar sound and vision, and to apply this sensitivity to the feelings in their own body. Adolescents and adults may be encouraged to relax and then to locate the sensations aroused in their bodies by particular thoughts or recollections, and reflect on what this may tell them.

Discovering emotional complexity through language

As we get older, our ability to be aware of and to distinguish our feelings is mediated by our ability to express them in words (Gardner 1993a; Greenberg and Snell 1997). So helping learners get in touch with their feelings is concerned with exploring and developing linguistic competence, while work with adults is usually heavily dependent on talk.

Language helps us to recognise complexity: feelings are rarely simple and consistent. We need to help young people, and some adults, to develop a more sophisticated vocabulary for their feelings, for example by replacing the simplistic 'I feel bad' with the more precise 'I feel confused and a bit apprehensive', or by changing the banal 'I love him' into the more accurate 'I find him irritating at times, but I do like the way he makes me laugh.' Adolescents, in particular, like to see the world in black and white, and will benefit from recognising and naming complex, confused and sometimes conflicting emotional states (Haviland-Jones *et al.* 1997). Language also help us in the ongoing struggle not to mistake one emotion for another, and to recognise when one feeling is behind a surface one, such as a deeper fear of rejection behind an immediate flash of anger. Words are helpful, too, to help us assess the intensity of our feelings. As we become more mature, we can appreciate that the emotions of ourselves and others can sometimes be false, exaggerated, feigned or manipulative. Emotions are never static, they change over time, so a further important ability is that of monitoring changes in how we feel, and recognising what triggers them in our own inner world (for example, tiredness, hormone changes), in our own physical actions (such as how active or slothful we are being, or what we have eaten or drunk) or in the outside world (such as other people's words or actions, the physical context, the weather or the time of day).

Accepting and expressing the full range of emotions

It is neither necessary nor wise to be afraid of any of our emotions, to deny their importance, or to be unable or unwilling to feel and express them. All the emotions, including the negative ones, are not only a fact of life, but are at root healthy and useful, even if we need to be able to limit some of their manifestations in some circumstances.

Emotion is by no means always the enemy of sensible thought and rationality. Mayer and Salovey (1997) suggest that the emotions often facilitate rational thought, allowing us to prioritise and direct attention towards what matters. Without emotional weighting, we have no way of deciding what course is better than another. Experiencing our own emotions enables us to empathise with others, to imagine how they are feeling, thus enabling us to understand them better and partly predict what they might do. Emotions help us to anticipate how we will experience an event, such as going to a new school or job, and thus help us make decisions about what to do, as well as to prepare for future happenings. Through an awareness of our changing feelings we can identify recurrent patterns in our life, and in our actions and reactions that may lead us to want to change them. So there are solid, rational reasons for being more emotionally sensitive.

We can only harness the energy, motivation and good sense that emotions can provide if we are able to acknowledge and express them. We are all the poorer as effective and fully rounded people if we do not allow ourselves truly to feel the force of our emotions. But in many school programmes that purport to develop mental, emotional and social health, there is an overwhelming emphasis on gaining control, on repressing feelings and acting cautiously and rationally. Being able to exercise control is indeed a vital competence as part of the overall picture, as we shall shortly see, but on its own it can become limiting, conservative and life denying. Studies that ask people to record their everyday mood changes suggest that most people do not experience intense emotions very often, but inhabit a 'grey' area in the middle of the emotional range most of the time (Diener and Larsen 1993). This is a long way from the 'positive state of well-being' that constitutes the WHO's (1946) most famous definition of health. So a key competence for mental, emotional and social health may well be to be able to feel the emotions appropriately, which in some cases may mean more often and more strongly. The aim of mental, emotional and social health education should not be blandness and over control, but understanding and accepting of the full range of emotions so we can harness them for positive good, rather than denying them.

Accepting and expressing negative emotion

An important developmental task is coming to acknowledge and accept the negative as well as the positive side of ourselves. All of us have a dark as well as a light side: managing to understand that dark side, and keep its destructive potential under control while using the energy it can provide in a positive and productive way is a challenge we must all master. The psychoanalysts, starting with Freud (1957), had the useful insight that we find it harder to acknowledge the darker side of ourselves, partly because we are told so often and from such an early age that it is unacceptable. As a result, we often attempt to bury such feelings as anger and violent impulses, and to hide them behind a mask of 'niceness'. Psychoanalysis has also usefully identified the common phenomenon of 'projection', in which we can push an unwanted part of our own personality or feelings onto someone else. This enables us safely to blame others for feelings we are refusing to recognise in ourselves. We may even unconsciously act out a behaviour that makes others behave in the way we are feeling. It is particularly important for teachers to recognise when such feelings are being projected by pupils rather than originating in the teacher, as this then provides powerful guidance as to the state of mind of the class or the individual pupil (Greenhalgh 1994). For example, if a particular group or pupil provokes a feeling of frustration in adults then the young people are probably frustrated and stuck themselves. Projection does not have to be negative, but can also be used benignly: the more the teacher feels calm, cheerful and in control of the situation the more their pupils begin to feel and act in the same way.

In coming to accept our negative emotions it may be helpful to realise that the problems we have today have an evolutionary basis (Seyle 1974). The instinctive physical reactions and urges to action that raw emotions produce were once highly useful in humans' past but are no longer as appropriate. For example, a sense of threat often provokes anger, which in turn produces a physical readiness to fight, which is highly useful against sudden attack by a predator, but which, in a modern context, can lead to violence and bullying of others. Alternatively, threat can provoke fear which, in a situation of physical threat, provides the good sense to run from the predator or to freeze, but, in the context of a psychological threat, can turn us into passive victims of other people's bullying, or set off chronic and disabling anxiety. The response of sad lethargy to loss and bereavement was useful to our wandering ancestors in causing them to feel like staying nearer to home in times of trauma rather than risk going away and running into more danger. Nowadays many of us are defeated by the chronic depression that loss can provoke.

Today we do not often need the more flamboyantly physical and expressive side of our emotional reactions, although they can still be very useful in a physical crisis, for example if we are mugged and have to run for our lives. However, we should not aim to eliminate these responses, but should channel them more appropriately. The impulses and reactions that strong feelings provoke can be useful. Powerful, positive feelings are obviously often best acted on: if you love someone, it is usually best to tell them so, and soon; if you enjoy doing something, it is sensible to do it as often as possible as long as it is not harmful to yourself or others. Strong negative feelings can also be useful goads: for example, anger may give us the courage to stand up for ourselves or others in the face of injustice; fear may give us the good sense to get out of relationships that are exploitive or abusive; a mild degree of anxiety can energise us into performing a task better; and sadness may help us take the time to mourn a loss, to recognise the significance of the lost person or object, and to reassess our goals and priorities.

Responding to negative feelings includes being able to express them strongly if you want to and have judged it appropriate, for example by giving strong voice to your anger or joy, or by crying freely to experience your sorrow. When we are low, frightened or angry, simply expressing our negative feelings can sometimes make us feel better without the need for any further intervention. It is especially helpful to realise that others feel them too, and that we are not uniquely mad, bad or sad. We may sometimes want to help timid, passive people acquire the courage to act to redress a wrong, even when to do so makes them frightened, to be more assertive about their own needs and on behalf of others when they would rather be passive, and to express their anger rather than turning it into self-blame. There is then a positive role for negative emotions as a guide to do what is right (Wilberg 1998).

Schools need to allow pupils to feel negative as well as positive emotions, and to help them find effective and non-destructive ways to express all of them. Expressing negative emotions may mean that we need to create 'safe areas' in the school where a child in an angry panic can go and if necessary ventilate his/her angry feelings by physical action (cushion hitting or running around) or noise (shouting or screaming), without disturbing others, and where they can eventually cool off. When encouraging children to express themselves creatively, through dance, art, writing and role-play, we need to allow them to express the dark as well as the light side of their natures. In any classrooms, or indeed staff-rooms, it is important to have 'safe' sessions when children and adults can moan about what they like, about the school or the class, with no recriminations. Most of all, people in emotional pain need someone to talk to one-to-one; someone who will really listen to them. We examine this most vital of competences in detail in the next chapter.

Expressing negative emotions to pupils

It is helpful if teachers occasionally talk to pupils about their own feelings, including the darker ones they may be experiencing at the time. If children never see or hear about the negative emotions of others, they may well conclude that they have to bear all the responsibility for having such feelings, which can be very destructive for their sense of self-worth (Winnicott 1984). Simply hearing people talk calmly about their own negative emotions helps pupils to realise that such feelings can be coped with, and responded to in reflective and constructive ways.

Similarly, although on the whole we want children to receive positive feedback from their teachers, it is important that adults sometimes express their negative assessments to children, albeit in a conscious, careful and controlled way, to give children a sense of realism in how they affect others. For example, pupils who teachers find irritating are often irritating to other pupils: if the teacher shares his/her reactions sensitively with the child, it may help the irritating child to reflect on their behaviour, understand why other children are responding to him/her as they do, and have the motivation to change.

Limiting and containing negative feelings

Having made a case for the experience and expression of negative feelings, it is necessary to sound a strong note of caution. Experiencing the negative emotions of others directed at you is usually hurtful and can be extremely destructive for self-esteem. If we encourage children to express their negative emotions, we must take care to make it safe for them and for others around them. Furthermore, research studies have long demonstrated that, contrary to popular belief, 'ventilating' negative feelings can be harmful, and can fuel or even create a problem rather than soothe (Mallick and Candless 1966). We need an overall strategy that both recognises negative feelings and allows for their expression, and which gives learners the capacity to move on rapidly from this point to manage their feelings. Expressing negative feelings can then become one option among many and, if appropriate, can be carried out with caution, thought, care and reflection, in the right place, at the right time, and with due awareness of its likely consequences.

We all need to learn to be able sometimes to limit negative emotions so that what starts as normal and appropriate reactions do not overwhelm us, and so we do not feel negative emotions too deeply, too intensely, or for too long (Rowe 1996; Seligman 1975; 1991; Kennerley 1997). For example, we may need to ensure that righteous anger does not slip over into violence, that appropriate sadness does not decline into chronic depression, or that useful arousal does not turn into a permanent state of anxiety. We need the ability to acknowledge, contain and use difficult feelings, and then move on from them, to shake them off and let go of them rather than ruminating or obsessing about them. Having acknowledged and managed our negative feelings, we can then exercise self-restraint when it is appropriate to do so, controlling impulses that would otherwise lead to action when that action could be damaging to ourselves and/or others. Psychologists who have studied early child development, in particular Bowlby (1980) and Winnicott (1964; 1984), see the ability to manage the emotions as basic to growth. They suggest that the ability to manage inner emotion through 'soothing oneself' is a fundamental skill that babies can learn while very young if they are looked after by effective carers: the babies then emulate the techniques of their carers, gradually internalising helpful actions to find ways to hang on to good feelings and let go of bad ones.

Managing anger

Anger is the mood that most people are worst at controlling. In the short term it prompts us to either fight or fly, but in the longer term the sense of arousal it provokes can take hours to dissipate. Anger is often cumulative, and if another provoking incident comes to us before our anger from the last one has gone, it can be amplified by the previous emotion, resulting in a 'last straw' explosion.

Fortunately, we have considerable knowledge of specific techniques that help people to manage anger. Goleman (1996) describes a simple sequence that can help all of us cope with immediate flashes of anger using competences that very much echo those we suggest in this chapter. He suggests we first need to recognise the physical sensations of anger and take it as a cue to stop escalating the situation, for example by breathing more deeply and/or walking away. If we catch ourselves or someone else in the early stage, it can be helpful to engage in positive self talk, reassessing the cause of the anger, examining whether it is appropriate, and thinking of other interpretations and ways of responding. This needs to be done early: done too late, it can just inflame the angry person. If the anger has taken hold, then a cooling-off period may help, perhaps with a distraction to prevent the person ruminating on the cause, which can simply feed the anger. Providing alternative physical outlets, such as cushion thumping, running, shouting or exercise, can be helpful in some cases and for some people, while in other situations or with other people calming techniques and physical relaxation are more helpful. Only when the person has calmed down is it sensible to return to whatever issue may have caused it, and attempt more calmly to find a way forward: we examine the similar sequences involved in conflict resolution in the next chapter.

Teaching these simple techniques of anger management has proved helpful for those working with ordinary people who suffer from the usual problems caused by anger, including in schools. Enger (1995) for example, carried out an evaluated study of violence prevention in middle years for all pupils, and found that all pupils gained in knowledge and skills, and that the number of disciplinary referrals was reduced. So all of us can benefit from education to help manage anger better.

Some people are, however, chronically angry, causing trouble and violence for themselves and others wherever they go. Such people may need more comprehensive help that tackles the problem at many levels, looking at a range of related attitudes, beliefs and behaviours in order to get to the root of what may be a complex and long-term problem (Furlong and Smith 1994; Ollech 1992). It would seem that for some habitually angry people the problem is cognitive and perceptual: they often appear to be suffering from a lack of empathy and social sensitivity, and have trouble interpreting the signs of others, seeing neutral or friendly gestures as hostile. Slaby and Guerra (1988) interviewed chronically angry pupils and found that they thought differently to others, for example, seeking fewer facts before acting, having less insight into alternative solutions and failing to anticipate the negative consequences of their behaviour. Teachers in the US have been particularly active in developing initiatives to help habitually angry pupils to manage their anger, teaching them to reframe their perceptions and reactions by using cognitive and behavioural approaches: Larson (1994) has reviewed a whole range of interventions that use a wide range of approaches with success.

Limiting impulsivity

A key part of managing our emotions, especially our anger, is getting a hold on the tendency most of us have to be impulsive (Brigham 1989; Grossman and Hughes 1992). Strong emotions tend to lead all of us to want to react immediately, but this is often not a good idea. Some children, particularly boys, have particular problems in being over-impulsive, which can lead to them having poor selective attention, a proneness to making errors, aggressive social behaviour, immaturity of moral reasoning, behaviour problems and deficient reading skills. Learning to control such impulsivity can lead to increased self-confidence and self-esteem (Lowenstein 1983). Sadly, it seems that in practice young people are getting worse at managing their own negative emotions: long-term surveys by Achenbach in the United States suggest that young people are exhibiting a worsening in over forty measures of their emotional and social competences, and are becoming, for example, more aggressive, impulsive, disobedient, lonely and sad (Goleman 1996). So the need for this work is ever more pressing.

Recent work on the brain has given us more insight into the problem of impulsivity: Goleman (1996) summarises this research under the term 'emotional hijacking', which describes the ability of the brain to respond immediately to a stimulus perceived as threatening and produce a powerful emotional and physical response before the rational mind has time to kick in, sometimes before we are consciously aware of what the event was.

Again, this response had a good deal of evolutionary usefulness in enabling humans to produce what in animals is known as the 'startle' response, and to fight or flee. In the kind of social situations in which modern humans finds themselves it can too easily lead at best to a sudden flash of verbal aggression which we later regret, or at worst to impulsive violence. So a simple but effective technique for enabling people to manage their emotions better is helping them sensitise to their 'emotional hijack' response, and become aware of the importance of leaving time for initial reactions to an event to subside somewhat before acting.

Becoming more rational about the emotions

Managing our own behaviour involves learning to think about our emotions more effectively (Nelson Jones 1989). For example, we can come to see the link between emotion and action as having several potential stages, each of which is distinct and potentially under our control. We come to realise that we can move from our initial feelings, turn them into more rational thought, consider a range of potential options, decide between them, and consider the potential outcomes. Once we have grasped the possibility of alternative courses of action and ways of thinking, we can anticipate the consequences of various types of action, decide which we most want and tailor our own behaviour accordingly (Dryden 1995). Language is again central to the process of achieving inner balance: as children mature and become more reflective and self-aware, their feelings come more and more under the potential control of their rational minds through the process often termed 'self talk' – in other words holding an inner dialogue, learning to think and talk about feelings, rather than having no option but to react to them and act them out (Greenberg and Snell 1997; Butler and Hope 1995). When we are aware of how we feel we are more able to distance ourselves from the immediate engulfment of the feeling, to monitor and reflect on ourselves, to be in some sense a friend to ourselves, hovering above the mood and observing ourselves neutrally. If children gain practice in such self-regulatory talk, for example in organised classroom activity, they gradually internalise the process, and it does not have to be so explicit: Hymans (1994) showed how useful learning positive self talk can be in reducing impulsive behaviour in the school context.

Self-motivation

Once we are more in control of our behaviour we have the ability to plan in the longer term, to shape our lives by setting ourselves short, medium and long-term goals, a series of small, gradual steps that build on each other and gradually and progressively lead to an ultimate aim. This ability to motivate ourselves to positive, long-term action has been called by Goleman (1996) the single most significant 'master' aptitude that holds the key to our own success or failure, and some are attempting to set up programmes in schools that teach self-motivation directly (Hartley-Brewer 1997).

Self-motivation is based on what some have called 'intentionality' (Goleman, 1996), the confident belief that you have the will and the way to succeed, are competent and effective, and can have an impact on the world. This is in turn dependent on having high self-esteem as it requires an optimistic outlook, holding to the belief that you will eventually succeed in the face of difficulties and setbacks and when faced with onerous jobs through persistency and the willingness to try again. It requires guarding against negative thought patterns, and replacing them with positive thoughts (Seligman 1991). Phares (1976), basing his ideas on those of Rotter, saw such attitudes as based on fundamental beliefs about power and fate. He felt that people differ as to whether they see what happens to them as determined by their own actions, or alternatively as being decided by forces external to themselves, such as other, more powerful people or some ill-defined 'fate'. He labelled these different perspectives as the possession of an 'internal' or an 'external' 'locus of control'. Those who locate control within themselves have been shown to be more effective, successful and happier in their lives, their relationships, their work, indeed in everything they attempt.

The influence of gender

Gender has some considerable influence over our social and affective health, and is especially relevant to the issue of emotional containment and expression. Many studies have shown that men find difficulty communicating their feelings (MacLeod and Barter 1998), preferring to talk about things and actions (Gray 1994), to compete, make jokes and 'score points' off each other. Girls and women are more sensitive to relationships, empathic, more expressive, more verbal, feel the emotions more intensely and with more volatility, and are more able to articulate their feelings (Goleman 1996). Girls are more likely to see happiness, unhappiness and self-esteem as coming from themselves and other people, while boys tend to see them as emanating from what they do and achieve, such as sporting success or failure (Gordon and Grant 1997).

Given the well-known association between bullying, physical violence and crime, and masculinity (Balding 1998; Smith 1995), boys are often seen as needing help to find appropriate ways to control their behaviour, especially their anger, and express it in non-active ways, through words rather than physical actions. Girls tend not to act out their feelings in such a physical way but, in contrast, when faced with difficulties and conflicts, and especially following trauma, will often become passive and 'frozen' (Herman 1994). Girls tend to blame themselves for the problem rather than blaming the other person or seeing things as a matter of chance. This is consistent with the evidence that girls have lower self-esteem and less confidence, are more likely to believe that events are outside of their control, and are less trusting and less assertive than boys (Balding 1998; Patterson and Burns 1990). So girls are seen as needing more help to value themselves more and acknowledge their right to their feelings, particularly socially unacceptable ones such as anger (Stanford and Donovan 1993; MacLeod and Barter 1988; Herman, ibid.). For example, Shendell (1992) in the US describes a small-group programme that attempted to provide girls with the necessary tools to express negative feelings, including anger, and thereby to achieve more effective and assertive communication, while in the UK a Sheffield group has produced a pack on building self-esteem in girls (Adams 1998).

So, the sexes have slightly different needs, and we need to bear this in mind when planning an educational strategy for emotional competence building. However, this difference should be seen as a difference in emphasis not kind. Girls can be competitive and bullying too, usually in invisible, interpersonal rather than physical ways, by excluding others from their close-knit groups and engaging in psychological terrorism (Lane 1989). Boys can be very self blaming, for example they are more prone to successful suicide than are girls (DoH 1992). So both sexes need to learn to both express and control their feelings according to need, to be in touch with their feelings of anger and able to voice them strongly and powerfully where necessary, or hold them back if needed and find alternative ways to relate to others.

Seeking happiness

We have spent considerable time on looking at how we can best react to the problems and issues raised by negative emotional states. But we need to remember that there is more to the development of mental, emotional and social health than this. Programmes that purport to help us to develop emotional intelligence often wind up being all about self-denial, self-control and the management of negative emotions, especially programmes that are intended for young people. Such programmes turn affective and social education into a rather dour and grim process, and thus not likely to be very attractive to the young. Education should also be about developing the action competences that will enhance positive emotions, such as happiness, joy, elation, love and concern, and to help us to experience more positive emotions in our lives.

Fortunately, there is a small but growing research effort into discovering how people can be helped to become more happy, and sustain the feeling for longer. It appears that a key aspect of being happy is again concerned with 'self talk', replacing negative with positive beliefs (Holden 1998; Seligman 1991; Argyle, Martin and Lu 1995): it includes losing puritanical theories about happiness, realising, for example, that it does not have to be deserved, paid for or earned. It also involves seeing that happiness comes from within you, not from what happens to you, and that it is possible to be happy right now, rather than conditional on some future event or state that never happens. You are responsible for your own happiness; it is not up to other people to make you happy; what others do does not have to make you unhappy; you can be happy whatever is going on around you; and happiness is not what happens to you, it is what you create for yourself within yourself.

Achieving happiness is not just a matter of mental work: what we do with our bodies has a profound experience on how we feel. Research suggests that we can improve our happiness levels by taking part in activities we enjoy and that make us feel good, especially those that involve vigorous physical exercise (Barr 1985), relaxation and meditation. Food is also very influential over mood, and the main benefit of a healthy diet is the feeling of energy and vigour it produces. Simply getting in the habit of smiling and laughing as often as possible can be a very powerful gloom dispeller and stress reducer.

Young people are highly motivated to seek immediate happiness, not defer gratification. Childhood and adolescence is a time of emotional highs and lows; young people have a strong tendency to live in the present, experience their emotions intensely, and in particular place great emphasis on the importance of fun and 'having a laugh' (Coleman and Hendry 1990). Compared with their teachers and parents, teenagers are more likely to live for today, go for the immediate thrill, enjoy risk and excitement and see 'having a good time' as a greater priority than serious work (Willis 1977; Gordon and Grant 1997). They are motivated by the immediate pay off, not the long-term goal. Such tendencies are sadly often seen by psychologists and educators alike as signs of immaturity, but the capacity for having fun is a vital action competence, essential to achieving happiness. It may well be that adults need to learn to regain it, rather than young people learn to curb it.

Happiness education relates to many aspects of mental, emotional and social education. For example, the drive young people have to take illegal drugs can be at least partly explained by what is at root a simple desire to feel good and happy, to have fun, to relax, to feel part of a friendly crowd, to forget yourself and leave the worries of the world behind for a while. It is the same drive that causes their parents to have a drink after a hard day, or use alcohol to get a social gathering going. Of course, like alcohol, the taking of illegal drugs can do harm, but we are unlikely to be able to prevent easily something that meets such a basic need in the young. We need to recognise the desire to get high, to feel ecstasy, to feel at home in your environment is at root a very positive and healthy one. So, one way forward, rather than to deny the impulse, is to work with young people on ways in which they can feel that good by other means. A key goal for mental, emotional and social health education then becomes to help people experience longer and more intense positive mood states, to consolidate the highs and avoid the lows, and to find ways to conjure positive mood states that are more under their own control and less dependent on external events and the taking of mind-altering substances, whether legal or illegal.

The good news is that if we want to foster happiness in the young we are starting with a very captive audience. The survey by Gordon and Grant (1997) found that when asked what made them happy, young people most often identified friends, with 'having a laugh' seen as a major contributor to such happiness. In some schools, humour and fun can be interpreted as annoying or threatening, and schools can be dour and humourless places. Although of course humour can be cruel and 'having a laugh' can get out of hand, nevertheless the urges that provoke it are healthy ones and should be encouraged. Both pupils and teachers need to acquire the skills to cope with laughter and jokes, not standing too much on their dignity, and allowing themselves to be ribbed within reason.

Going with the flow

We have said that education, including mental, emotional and social health education, can sound worthy but grim, involving the kind of hard work, planning and deferment of gratification that none could keep up for long. Thus presented it can sound extremely demotivating, especially for the young and fun-seeking. Fortunately, there is a useful mechanism that kicks in at a certain point, which takes us to a different level altogether, and which is intrinsically delightful. A sense of 'flow' has been reported by many who are engaged in a task in which they are very skilled, from painting, to playing music, to sports (Csikszentmihalyi 1990). Flow is a state of total attention and immersion in the task, a forgetting of the self, a turning out of an excellent performance with apparently no effort. It is accompanied by an inner sense of transcendental joy, rapture, peace and mild ecstasy. Studies of the brain show that it quietens while flow is occurring, and only works as needed. Flow is then the opposite of a state of strained concentration.

There is certainly no escaping the fact that flow is the product of the '99 per cent perspiration' of which Einstein claimed genius was made: flow does not welcome us easily and without prior effort. It is experienced by those who already have a good degree of the necessary skill, who then face themselves with a task that is a little more difficult than usual. In a state of flow, the challenge is then reward: the activity becomes an end in itself with no need for extrinsic motivation. Experiencing flow is a powerful incentive to carry on with the activity, and to try to find it again. So, perhaps we would better motivate young people by teaching them to tap into a sense of flow, found through doing what they love and can do well, rather than constantly presenting education as a process of gaining extrinsic rewards through examination grades or a good job, achieved solely through 'hard graft' and self-denial.

Emotions in the school

During the course of this chapter we have discussed some of the ways in which schools can help learners to become more emotionally literate, but there are a few more general observations to make about teachers' emotional competences, and about the place of emotion in school.

Teachers' emotions

The teacher has a vital role in 'emotional holding' (Winnicott 1984), by which is meant demonstrating that disturbing feelings have a meaning, and can be tolerated, managed, reflected on and understood; they do not have to possess you, take you over, cause you to react blindly. It is then essential that teachers themselves are stable, calm and consistent if they are to be good role models for their pupils in managing their emotions. As the older, if not always the more mature, partners in the process, teachers need to become extremely self-aware of their own emotional reactions, recognising that they are part of the total picture, not neutral observers of their pupils' needs and development.

If they are to claim to be of help to others, it is particularly essential that teachers have a high degree of awareness of their own feelings, including accepting their own darker side. Acknowledging the side of ourselves we do not much like helps all of us to reduce our own judgmentalism and increase our empathy with others. It reminds us how difficult and complex feelings can be, and helps us overcome our usual professional response of pretending there are easy answers to complex problems. Being sensitive to our own reactions also helps us to retain the proper distance, control and boundaries. Without such awareness it is all too easy for the feelings of the child or young person to trigger our own unconscious or unsorted emotions and problems. For example, a teacher who has his/her own anger triggered by witnessing a child's violent explosions may only be able to think of punitive solutions: recognising and accepting his/her own anger may help the teacher, and thus the pupil, to think of other solutions.

For some teachers, working with the young can raise powerful emotions that can get in the way of being effective. Some adults who have never quite grown up themselves cannot provide effective boundaries because they cannot distance themselves sufficiently from pupils, but instead over-identify with them, gain vicarious enjoyment from their emotional problems, and feel the powerful pull of regression (Greenhalgh 1994). Those teachers who have not come to terms with their own sense of loss for missed opportunities may in contrast find it hard to identify with the young, becoming instead overly moralistic with those young people they perceive as 'throwing away' opportunities by not working hard or who take risks with their health.

Incorporating emotion into the everyday life of the school and classroom

If the school ethos is to support work on emotional health, then schools, classrooms and staff-rooms need generally to become more comfortable with discussing feelings and emotions. Children and teachers need to feel that they are as permitted and encouraged to talk about their feelings as they are about their knowledge, skills or intellectual understanding. Given that children, and even more adolescents, are primarily emotional, and usually very interested in their own feelings and those of their friends, incorporating emotion should make the teacher's job easier by going with the flow of what pupils want to do anyway (Elias *et al.* 1997). It helps pupils to internalise their learning and to make it relevant and meaningful to their everyday concerns. We can stop fighting the emotional side of pupils, and teachers, and instead integrate it into the classroom and the staff-room, connecting the personal with the academic.

For example, pupils can be encouraged at regular intervals to monitor and discuss how they are feeling right now, or how they felt when something happened recently. They can be encouraged to discuss what they could or should do about that feeling. When reflecting on what they have learned at school, at the end of a lesson, or at the end of term, pupils and teachers can be encouraged to include discussion of their feelings, to reflect on how these feelings changed, as well as clarifying what they have learnt in the way of facts, processes or skills. Real-life incidents, such as the introduction of a new pupil into the class or a new teacher into the school, incidents of bullying or nerve-wracking school inspections, provide opportunities to help pupils and teachers develop their emotional and social competences, for example, by recognising and talking about their feelings and listening to those of other people, exploring a range of ways forward in a situation, and practising different solutions.

However, as Mayer and Salovey (1997) point out, we need to be aware that not all cultures and social groups are equally at ease in exploring the emotions: in some cultures stoicism, particularly for boys, and/or 'turning the other cheek' may be the norm; it may also come hard to some older teachers who were brought up in a more emotionally contained climate. We need to remember that some children may find work on the sharing of feelings or being asked to disclose personal information about themselves or their families clashes with the cultural values of the home, where such discussions and disclosures are seen as inappropriate (Elias 1990). Emotional and social education needs to address the diversity of ways of learning and cultural norms, and be sensitive to differences that are rooted in ethnicity, culture and age. So it may be best not to press those pupils or teachers for whom the discussion of emotions is unfamiliar or uncomfortable, but find safe and possibly private ways for all those who are not happy with public discussion of their feelings to express themselves without feeling exposed or uncomfortable. Younger children, for example, could use anonymous 'feeling boxes' into which they 'post' written expressions of their feelings; older pupils may prefer role-play in which they can hide behind a character, or write a dialogue for other people to say; teachers may prefer to be consulted on a one-to-one basis.

Conclusions

This chapter has examined the central importance of self-esteem and the building of a realistic self concept to mental, emotional and social health, and looked at the wide range of competences that are needed if we are to understand and express our emotions better, and be more emotionally intelligent and literate. The next chapter will look at how we can move on to use those intra-personal competences in what is for most of us the main pleasure in life, making and keeping warm personal relationships. The final chapter will suggest more specific ways in which emotional and social competences can be transmitted through the taught curriculum.

4 Developing social competency

Goals of this chapter

This chapter looks at the social competences we need to relate effectively to others, and at how schools can best promote them. It first explores three key attributes, empathy, respect and genuineness, which underlie all social competency, then looks at the active listening skills that can help us realise those attributes in practice, and at how schools can encourage more effective listening. It looks at a range of competences that relate to our ability to be more social, such as making friends, being effective in a group, being assertive, being our own person and tolerating others. Finally, it examines the issue of managing conflict, in which some of the processes and competences that have been discussed so far come together.

Making relationships

The centrality of relationships

In many ways the distinction between the personal focus of the last chapter and the more social focus of this chapter is one of convenience only, as it is in practice difficult to separate emotional and social competences. Relationships are not just what happens to us, as we ourselves have a profound influence over how others relate to us: even very young babies have been shown to differ in their abilities to elicit caring from their parents (Bowlby 1980). It is possible to be more or less competent at making relationships, to exhibit what Gardner (1993a) has called 'interpersonal intelligence', which is the social ability to understand others and how to cooperate with and be understood by them. This social intelligence is another crucial meta-ability that governs our success and levels of fulfilment in virtually all aspects of our lives, from making friends to holding down a job (Goleman 1996). Fortunately, it can very much be learned.

The relationship between emotional and social competency works the other way too, and experiencing warm personal, trustworthy relationships is absolutely fundamental for the growth of self-esteem. Young people realise the importance of relationships only too well and relationships are clearly of the utmost importance to them, even more so than they are to older people who may have acquired some degree of detachment and self-sufficiency. Gordon and Grant (1997) found that, when asked what made them happy, young people most commonly cited 'other people', with half of them mentioning friends and one in seven mentioning family. Similarly, 'other people' was the most commonly cited cause of unhappiness, with one-fifth mentioning friends and one in nine mentioning their families as a source of unhappiness.

Empathy

Carl Rogers (1983) suggests that three key competences underpin our ability to make caring relationships: they are the capacity for empathy, genuineness and respect. He carried out a good deal of work on the centrality of these issues for schools, and claims that they are fundamental to any programme of affective and social education, for pupils or teachers. He also sees them as underpinning the academic and professional life of the school, maintaining that the higher the levels of empathy, genuineness and respect that the teacher gives to the pupils, the more the pupils will learn. The same applies to staff: the more they feel understood, respected and know where they stand, the more effort they will put into their work and supporting the life of the school.

Having empathy means that you try to understand other people and how they 'tick', to see the world from the other person's point of view, and to put yourself in their shoes. To be genuinely empathic, such understanding needs to be for the whole person, not just the bits you like about them or that you wish to see. Empathy is not the same as sympathy: sympathy implies that your own feelings are necessarily aroused, and often results in a confusion between your own feelings and those of the other person. Empathy, in contrast, can be more dispassionate but is potentially more useful: it demands that you see things from the other person's point of view, not your own, that you separate yourself from them and do not become over involved or indulge in transference of feelings. A key part of empathy is realising that someone else can feel very differently to you about something but still deserve your concern and understanding.

The requirement of empathy returns us to the need for self-knowledge, self-esteem and self-acceptance. We cannot distinguish ourselves from others unless we have a clear view of our own feelings, their origins, their complexity, their contradictions, and how we feel, think and react. We cannot easily extend acceptance and tolerance to others if we do not accept and tolerate ourselves. In attempting to understand another we may sometimes have to recognise feelings in ourselves that we had not been acknowledging. Being with others empathically tends to cause us to realise that we are all more like each other than we sometimes care to admit.

Empathy is a central competence for teachers dealing with troubled or troublesome pupils (Hayden 1997). We have argued that we need to be looking for the meaning behind the behaviour, and attempt to understand its root causes (Elton 1989), but often troublesome or troubled behaviour is, at first sight, meaningless to an outsider. The biggest barrier to empathy, and thus to helping someone learn or change, is the belief that you cannot understand what they do, that their behaviour is in some way incomprehensible or outside of normal human experience. The wise teacher will assume that apparently mystifying behaviour has some point from the pupil's point of view, some inner logic, or pay off, and seek to discover it. It can help to bear in mind that all behaviour has a history and a context in which it originated, and in which it makes or made sense (Mayer and Salovey 1997). As Lowenstein (1983) suggests, children can continue to practice a demeanour that may have been necessary for their early survival, but is inappropriate in later circumstances. For example, if a child experiences the key adults in his/her early life as unloving or untrustworthy, the child will tend to extend this belief to all adults in later life. Pupils who have been let down a good deal in the past by parents or by other teachers may have learned that trust is dangerous, and many engage in lengthy 'testing out' of new teachers, which they carry on to the limit before they feel safe. Children from such backgrounds are also more likely to bully others (Bowers *et al.* 1994).

Empathy is one of the most vital forces holding society together: it is the root of compassion and the fundamental 'people competence'. Hoffman (1984) has argued that the roots of morality lie in empathy and that those without it can become psychopaths and sociopaths. As we have seen, habitually angry young people often find it difficult to see things from another person's point of view, and interpret friendly or neutral behaviour as aggressive (Slaby and Guerra 1988; Goleman 1996). So many programmes that attempt to combat bullying include working with those who bully others to help them imagine the situation from the victim's perspective (Rigby 1997). Some anti-bullying programmes have taken this pursuit of empathy even further, seeing it as essential that teachers and other concerned adults also understand the problems of the bully and, while not condoning bullying, use the so-called 'non-blame' approach (Robinson and Maines 1997). Lack of empathy is also often to be found at the root of the problems of children who are isolated and friendless, who are thus more likely to be the victims of bullying. We shall shortly discuss such asocial 'dyssemic' children in some detail. So, learning to be more empathic can alleviate a wide range of problems experienced by children and young people, as well as, more positively, making the school into a place where all feel valued and supported.

Genuineness

Rogers' second key human value is genuineness. Genuineness is another word for authenticity: it implies congruence between how you seem to others and what you are inside, not presenting a façade or a defence, not pretending to be other than what you are, or claiming to feel, believe or do what you do not. Genuineness means that you can be trusted to be what you appear, to keep your word, and not promise what you cannot deliver. Again, it is clear that genuineness has to be based on thorough self-understanding: you have first to know who you 'really' are before you can show that face to others without too many subterfuges and defences. When you are genuine you are able to be open about your own feelings, to engage with others, to react fully, and to listen and respond with the whole of yourself.

Genuineness is strongly related to the key principle of clarity, which we discussed earlier. Genuineness is a particularly vital attribute for those who work with children and young people. The young seem to have in-built detectors of any kind of inauthenticity or phoniness, and give the most respect where they find the most genuineness. Openness and a willingness to look at feelings, including uncomfortable ones, is an essential part of working effectively with young people. Genuineness enables adults not to get sucked into young people's issues but to keep their own boundaries, and boundaries are, as we have seen, vital to help young people feel safe (Greenhalgh 1994). Attempting to be genuine reminds adults of the need not to collude or try to relive their youth through young people, but to be very clear that they are separate and different generations. Genuineness is also a foundation for helping other people by giving us the ability to provide accurate feedback on how they are experienced by those around them: it may well be that the teacher is the only person in the young person's life who can provide this genuine feedback in a safe and supportive way.

Respect

Rogers' third and final key attribute is respect, which he also sometimes called acceptance or prizing. Respect means demonstrating that you think the other person is important, worthwhile, valuable and unique.

Being able to demonstrate respect is the ability that enables us to give the unconditional positive regard that is, as we have seen, fundamental for the fostering of self-esteem. It is concerned with caring about someone and approving of them as a person, even if not always condoning or colluding with their overt behaviour. Providing such unconditional positive regard is a vital way for teachers to help those with low self-esteem to build it: it gives pupils the belief that they can be better, and that they will change. This is again particularly important when working with difficult pupils, where the task of the teacher is often to 'hold the faith' that the child can be better on his/her behalf when the child cannot find that belief within themselves (Winnicott 1984). This may be the first stage in helping the pupil to learn to believe in themselves.

Listening and responding effectively

The centrality of listening

There is no point in just feeling empathy, respect and genuineness for others: without the action competences to communicate them, these qualities stay locked inside ourselves, and are of little use to anyone. To be made real they have to be demonstrated to others.

The basis of all relationships is communication, the exchange of feelings, ideas and concepts with others, verbally and non-verbally (Argyle 1985). The most basic and important skill in communication is not, as many people think, talking, but listening (Burley-Allen 1982). As the old Hebrew saying puts it, 'the beginning of wisdom is silence', so one of the most powerful ways in which we can demonstrate our empathy, genuineness and respect is through actively listening to others. Being listened to in an active way is a wonderful experience. Having the undivided, unconditional attention of another person is excellent for self-esteem: it makes us feel interesting, worthwhile and understood (Coopersmith 1967). When you are listened to, you begin to listen to and understand yourself better, start to recognise lovable parts of yourself, accept the less lovable parts, and see yourself as more able to change.

Listening is the single best way to help those in emotional difficulties

Listening is absolutely vital when it comes to helping those in difficulties. Many of those who have had experience in working with people with mental, emotional or social problems inevitably conclude that the single most important action anyone can take is to encourage the sufferer to talk, listen to what they say and try to understand his/her experience (Burningham 1994) The central importance of listening to the young person and understanding his/her point of view has been emphasised time and again by those with experience of working to help children and young people going through crises, such as loss and bereavement (Wolfelt 1983; Dyregrov 1990), or with more established mental health problems, such as depression (Cytryn 1997), suicidal feelings (Shamoo and Patros 1990; Leenaars and Wenckstern 1991), eating disorders (Buckroyd 1996) or self harm (Herman 1994). Anyone can listen actively: you do not need to be a professional psychotherapist to be of simple help to the person with a problem.

Active listening is so central to the promotion of mental, emotional and social health that we will take some time to look at the competences that constitute it, as they are essential for all teachers and pupils to acquire.

Active listening

To listen effectively we need to do more than just 'be there' physically. Being able actively to listen to someone is a complex action competence, and active listening is not as easy as it appears: there is a wide range of skills that we need to exhibit and practise (Burley-Allen 1982). Few of us are born listeners. Our natural egocentrism means that very often we are not so much listening to someone else as waiting for them to stop talking so we can speak ourselves. We may not really hear what they are saying, but prefer to hear what we would like them to be saying. Even if we think we are listening, we may not be showing it: we may be looking around us, fidgeting or making it clear in other ways that we would rather be doing something else, all of which will make the other person feel as if they are not worth listening to.

Active listening requires that we make the other person feel that we are really listening to them, valuing them, and understanding what they have to say. It is essential not to interrupt or assume that we know what the other person is going to say, but instead allow the person to finish what they have to say in their own time and in their own way. Active listening is non-judgemental: we only really talk freely when we feel that what we say is accepted, and are not worried that the listener is seeing us as, for example, silly or wicked. There are a range of ways in which we can demonstrate our acceptance and valuing of the other person, non-verbally as well as verbally, and we examine them next.

Using body language effectively

We have said a good deal about the importance of language in developing mental, emotional and social competences, but when it comes to communicating with others, verbal language is surprisingly unimportant. Up to 90 per cent of the messages we send each other are non-verbal (Pease 1981). The basis of our ability to communicate non-verbally with others begins in infancy, long before we have language, when we start to learn to recognise cues from people's facial expressions, their tone, their body position and actions (Ekman *et al.* 1972).

So paying active attention is not just a matter of hearing the words that the other person is saying: we need to be sensitive to non-verbal clues, such as the amount of eye contact a person is prepared to accept, their appearance, expressiveness, gestures, and so on – all of which can tell us far more about that person's state of mind than what he/she is able or willing to put into words. Similarly, listeners themselves communicate far more about their attitudes though what they do than through what they say. Our body language can demonstrate concern or disregard, interest or lack of it, hostility or welcome, whatever our words may be saying. If we want to respond to people effectively, we need to take control of our own body language. We convey a sense of interest and acceptance of what the other person is saying by simple gestures and noises such as 'go on', 'uh huh', 'anything else?', by smiling, looking interested, and nodding. It is generally appropriate to turn to the speaker and use a reasonable amount of eye contact, although some people, especially the young, can find this overwhelming, and talk best when they and the listener are side by side, perhaps engaged in a joint activity. Whichever stance we use, we need to show that we are focusing on the person by keeping still and by remaining as physically close as both are happy with – a distance that may again vary according to age and cultural or social background (Watson 1972).

We also can demonstrate attention through 'sympathetic' responses, such as smiling when the other person smiles, frowning when they frown, and leaning towards them when they disclose a confidence. Taking this further, we can learn to 'mirror'. 'Mirroring' involves matching the other person's gestures with our own – sitting or standing in the same way as the other person, leaning forward or back when the other person does, turning towards the other person to make a pair of human 'bookends', and so on (Pease 1981). We all tend to 'mirror' the other person unconsciously when we are trying to impress them, for example if we are talking to our boss or chatting to someone with whom we want to strike up a friendship. It would seem that subconsciously we believe that someone who is mirroring our gestures understands us. So a useful skill in communicating effectively with others is to know how to mirror their body language, consciously and deliberately. It follows too that if we are trying to encourage someone to open up, we need to guard against unwittingly driving him/her away through discordant, defensive or even hostile body language, such as folding our arms across our chest when the other person says something we find threatening, or turning our body away from him/her when he/she has made a disclosure we find discomforting.

We can also use our own non-verbal and body language to try to change the mood of the speaker. We may, for example, attempt to de-escalate conflict by using a softer tone, calmer gestures, less threatening body language and fewer inflammatory words than the person we are talking to. We know we are succeeding in such attempts when the body language of the other person starts to mirror ours. Being able to use non-verbal and body language with control is a basic skill that we all need to master, and is particularly vital for teachers with their need to manage the behaviour and emotions of large groups of pupils.

Listening to give help and support

We have said that the experience of being listened to by someone who is giving you their full and obvious attention is very therapeutic. It is often enormously helpful as a way of sorting out our own problems, indeed sometimes no further help is needed (Carkuff 1985). Active listening has then a particularly central role in helping someone else with their problems. The ability really to listen to what each person is saying, take it seriously and value the contribution may be the vital first step in achieving their consent and willingness to change.

However, listening to provide help and support is again a highly skilled process (Egan 1998; Nelson Jones 1993). Very often, when we are keen to help a person who is talking about problems or difficulties, we find it hard to let them speak for long enough to begin to find their own solutions. In our eagerness to be 'helpful' we may offer premature advice, which may not be appropriate, and which may disempower a person who simply wanted to talk or be helped to come to his/her own conclusions. Active, empathic and respectful listening is not about providing instant solutions, giving unwanted and unsolicited advice, or engaging in moralising, lecturing, nagging or evaluating. One of the most important ways in which we solve problems is to work things out for ourselves, often simply through hearing ourselves talk in the presence of an empathetic listener (Nelson Jones 1989). The person with the problem may well not need advice, he or she may just need to have a listener to encourage them to speak: hearing ourselves articulating our thoughts is often enough to make us feel better about a difficulty, or see a way through a problem.

Responding effectively

We have said that the experience of just talking and being listened to is surprisingly helpful for our self-esteem and ability to solve problems. However, after a while, we often want to know what the person we are talking to thinks and feels about what we are saying. In learning to help others, we need to learn the competences of responding effectively and in a way that reinforces rather than undermines the sense of empathy, respect and genuineness we are trying to build up (Nelson Jones 1993).

A key component of our ability to make an effective response is the ability to concentrate on the main issues from the respondent's point of view. The listener needs to stay focused, and not respond to distractions, get lost in detail, engage in point scoring, make judgements, or indulge their own emotional needs. Offering prescriptive 'if I were you I would ... ' is usually not appropriate: it may make the person who is suggesting feel effective, but it rarely helps the person with the problem.

One useful response is that of reflecting back, which is about telling the speaker what you think you are hearing. Simply summing up or para-phrasing, as accurately as you can, what the speaker said can be a useful technique for validating what he/she is saying: it can also help them think more clearly. Simply repeating the last part of what the speaker said, provided it is not done to excess, can encourage them to talk further. It is certainly best to avoid lengthy interruptions if we want to encourage the other person really to open up. Going further, it may be appropriate to comment on how a person says something, for example whether they sound angry or frightened, but such second order analysis and commentary needs to be done sparingly and with caution. It is important to stick with what the person is telling you and work with that, rather than over interpreting and trying to play the amateur psychoanalyst.

Clarifying can be useful too. Clarifying involves asking the speaker to tell us more about something he/she has mentioned and that we think might be helpful to explore further, such as 'Could you tell me more about what you mean when you say you think that the teacher doesn't like you?' Other than that, it is advisable to be sparing in the use of questions. We need always to ask ourselves why we are asking a question: is it to satisfy our own needs and curiosity, or is it to help the person talking to go in the direction that feels right for them? We need to be careful to avoid interrogating.

Making active listening more central in schools

Being able to forget ourselves for a while and really listen to others is clearly a vital competence that few of us possess sufficiently, and which most of us need to practice a good deal more than we do. It is a key social competence for children and young people to learn, to help to mitigate their natural tendency to egotism, to start to become more social, to make friends and to be effective in groups. It also has, as we shall shortly see, a central role in resolving and mediating conflict.

So listening is one of the most central competences in promoting mental, emotional and social health, and needs to be active and non-judgemental. However, schools are often places where many talk but few listen. Research shows that in most lessons teachers talk a great deal and, in particular, ask a great many closed questions, although we certainly cannot conclude from this that the pupils are listening (Wood 1992). Pupil talk in class tends to be dominated by a few outgoing pupils, and some pupils may go through their school careers saying almost nothing to a teacher in class (Maclure *et al.* 1988).

Pupils may not be good at listening to each other: children and teenagers can be very egocentric, and the talking in the peer group too may again be dominated by a few confident young people. In some homes, conversation, particularly of the supportive and non-judgemental kind, may not be the norm, and some pupils may literally have no one in whom they can confide. For these pupils, 'a listening school' may be a lifeline.

Good schools may be skilled in helping pupils talk effectively about intellectual and cognitive matters, but many still do not have any organised and routine ways of encouraging pupils to talk about sensitive personal matters, either in class or privately. We have said that effective listening needs to be non-judgemental, but teachers spend most of their time evaluating pupils' work and therefore find it very hard to avoid being prescriptive in their reactions to what pupils tell them: for most teachers judgement is an ingrained habit. Of course, many teachers are skilled at helping pupils talk, including about personal matters, and know that the pupil who stays behind after class 'to help clear up' may have something on his/her mind that he/she wants to talk about in privacy. Some schools have found it useful to employ counsellors to talk to pupils in confidence about their problems (Geldard and Geldard 1997; WHO 1997b). What is needed is for schools to take a more systematic approach, and to ensure that all pupils have someone to whom they can talk easily, in private and in confidence (White 1995; Mind 1997). Encouraging all teachers and pupils to learn the competences of active listening, and to use them really to listen to each other would do a great deal to improve the mental and emotional health of everyone in the school community. It would be helpful, too, if all schools could find ways to help pupils explore their feelings, needs and problems as a routine and common part of school life. We explore ways in which this might become more of a reality in the final chapter.

Teachers may also need to work on the quality of their talk to each other. In some schools, staff gatherings may be occasions where there is not much productive, positive talk. Quite often staff-rooms are places where the disillusioned grumble for example, about the head, the pupils, the amount of work they feel they are asked to do, or the conditions they have to work under. Meanwhile, the more active, positive members of staff may be getting on with preparing and marking work, but in isolation from each other. Staff meetings may be top down exercises, with the head making a speech about the latest plan or problem, while some staff day-dream and others wait for the head to finish talking so they can take up the well-rehearsed positions they always take on any issue. Not all staff-rooms are like this of course, but many schools contain elements of this kind of dysfunctional communication. In many schools, staff as well as pupils would benefit from learning really to listen and communicate with each other.

We have taken some time to look at listening as it is so vital to promoting social and affective health, including helping people who are in distress. We will look now at some further basic social competences, and at how schools can promote them.

Becoming more socially competent

Making friends

Peer relationships, and particularly close friendships, are vital to our sense of self-esteem (Duck 1983). They provide the social context within which we can relax and have fun, challenge ourselves, learn new ideas and engage in new experiences. They increase our sense of self-worth through the sharing and reinforcing of our own thoughts and ideas. When as children we start to make friendships we realise, probably for the first time, that we possess certain beliefs, qualities and experiences in common with others. Friends are invaluable too in times of stress and emotional upset through listening, sharing and offering a shoulder to cry on, and providing good advice.

A child or young person without at least one close friend is deprived of the opportunity of such close communication, and his or her self concept suffers as a result: with no such friend to turn to for support and comfort, such children and young people often feel extremely lonely and even depressed (Rosenthal 1993). In general, unpopularity in childhood is a strong predictor of our emotional, social, and even material, success in later life, so it is vital that we all learn such basic social skills at a young age. Unfortunately, the ability to make relationships is by no means automatic for any of us, and some of us find it very difficult indeed. It has been estimated that as many as one child in ten has what amounts to a social learning deficiency: they find it very hard to relate to others and make friends: indeed psychologists have invented a term for this, 'dyssemia' (Nowicki and Duke 1992). Dyssemic children have poor empathetic skills: they do not seem to know how to act appropriately in social situations and have limited and isolating responses to others. They are basically not fun to be with, and do not know how to make the other person feel good, being for example more likely to sulk, brag, cheat and give up when losing. They are particularly poor at the empathetic skills that are vital for so many aspects of social relationships, and poor at demonstrating the vital competences of understanding and controlling body language which, as we have seen, is more significant in communication than words. They do not know how to read other people's signs, facial expressions and postures, for example, they often stand too close or too far away, and themselves give out inappropriate non-verbal signals. As a result they become socially isolated, angry, frustrated and often suffer academically as a result.

As well as the ability to make close friendships, it is also important, especially for adolescents, to know how to get along with and hold one's own in a group. Schools are places where a great deal of group interaction takes place, in the classroom, in the playground and in the staff-room. The world of work is nowadays largely based on working in groups and teams, where we may not like everyone as a friend, but within which we have to learn to operate effectively. So we all need to learn to feel comfortable and effective in groups, which is often more demanding than making friendships on a one-to-one basis.

Dyssemic children often have the same problems with groups as they have one to one. A particular characteristic of such children is that they tend to rush into social situations and behave in a way that disrupts the group and which results in them being excluded. In contrast, more socially skilled children are better at what could be termed 'social analysis' – the ability to be sensitive to what is going on in a group. When finding themselves in the position of outsider they will first watch others and work out what they are doing before making a cautious initial approach and joining in with the current activity without fuss. Thus, they gradually work their way to the inside of the group. The ability and willingness to work out what others are doing and to tailor behaviour, including body language, to the prevailing group norm is of course just as necessary for adults trying to gain acceptance, for example, with their new work-mates when starting a job.

Once accepted by a group, there is a range of action competences that need to be acquired and practised. Groups require that different people play different roles, and having a sense of what those roles need to be, and which is the most appropriate for you, is a highly useful action competence. There are action competences too concerned with self-disclosure, in other words telling the people something about yourself. We need to learn to gauge when it is safe to disclose, and what level of disclosure is appropriate in the circumstances, given our relationship with the other people and their level of interest in us.

Fortunately, work that has attempted to teach dyssemic children how to be more social has proved to be highly effective, while all children can gain from having their friendship skills polished. We will take just two examples (both from the US). Macklem (1987) describes a school-based, short-term intervention for teaching isolated children how to engage in play with other children. The technique involved teaching children how to recognise whether a group is open to newcomers, getting them to compile ideas for entering a group, role-playing, and having them practise their skills in the playground, and was used successfully with a wide range of age groups: from first to fifth grade, both boys and girls. Rosenthal (1993) describes a further successful project aimed at helping friendless children which used group work and social skills education approaches both with the child with difficulties and with the surrounding group.

Being assertive

As well as fitting in with others, we need to be able to express our own needs. People who attend only to the needs of others can become social chameleons, just fitting in with others, trying to impress everyone in an inauthentic way. In our everyday life, relationships and conversations are generally reciprocal affairs that involve an exchange of ideas, opinions and experiences. So a key action competence in making authentic relationships is balancing our own needs with those of others, and engaging in relationships that are mutually supportive and enlivening, an ability that some have called 'cooperativeness' (Goleman 1996). In improving cooperativeness, the concept of 'assertion' has proved particularly useful as it provides both a well-thought through set of principles and some specific skills through which to put these principles into practice (Fodor 1992).

Certain key values and attitudes underlie assertiveness, perhaps the most fundamental of which is seeing yourself and the other person as equally important, as having the same rights, and demanding the same respect and attention. The goal in assertive communication is for everyone to get something from a situation: for example, if there is a conflict of interest between you and another, the desired outcome is 'win/win'. This assertive attitude can be contrasted with having a passive attitude towards the other person, where you put yourself second and see the other person as more important, and are content if 'you win/I lose'. At the other end of the spectrum, and equally unhealthy, is the aggressive attitude (with which assertiveness is sometimes unfortunately confused), where you think that you are more important than the other, and in which 'I win/you lose' is the goal. This kind of 'me first' attitude does indeed often lead to literally aggressive behaviour, such as shouting or violence, but it can be expressed in other, more manipulative ways, so the word 'aggressive' in the context of assertion theory has a rather specialised meaning. Assertion is then a useful middle way between passivity and aggression, and as relevant for those without enough self-esteem as for those who, appear at least, to have too much.

Changing long-held patterns of aggressive or passive behaviour is not easy. Feeling assertive, and communicating that assertiveness, through words and, more crucially, appropriate body language involve a range of constituent competences which, for most people, takes a good deal of learning and practice. We will give just a few examples of key assertiveness skills here. One crucial principle is taking responsibility for your own behaviour rather than blaming others or trying to guess what they want. This can be conveyed, for example, by learning to give what have been called 'I' messages, in other words verbally owning your own emotions and actions. So, in place of the rather aggressive statement 'you make me angry', we could use the more assertive 'I feel angry when you do that'. The advantage of the second response is that it does not blame, or attempt to guess what the other person is thinking or intending, but on the other hand it gives them clear and indisputable information to which they can then decide how to respond. Saying 'no' clearly without feeling guilty and without causing offence is something that many people find difficult and takes a good deal of practice (Smith 1975). A further skill is handling criticism assertively, which involves listening carefully to what is said, accepting what you feel is, on reflection, true, and rejecting what you feel is unfair.

A good deal of effort has been put into teaching the attitudes and skills of assertiveness in a wide variety of contexts. Role-play with feedback has proved to be a particularly useful method, and is used in most initiatives. For some time now there has been a wide range of books and teaching materials available for teaching such skills to adults (Alberti and Emmons 1974), especially to women (Dickinson 1982). More recently, the concept of assertiveness has been applied in a school context, and has proved to improve the personal and social skills of a wide variety of pupils, including mainstream pupils who are not especially troublesome or troubled, but who have the normal range of problems in getting along with others (Buell and Snyder 1981; Huey and Rank 1984; Caplan *et al.* 1992; Fodor 1992). Assertiveness has also been applied to pupils with particular needs, and has proved useful, for example, in improving the self-esteem of black pupils (Stewart and Lewis 1986), and reducing aggression in pupils with behavioural problems (Dong *et al.* 1979). Indeed, the principles behind assertiveness have proved to be one of the bedrocks for reducing aggression and disputes in school – a vital issue we look at in more detail in relation to conflict and mediation later in this chapter.

Tolerating difference

We have suggested that mental, emotional and social health includes the ability to get along with others, to fit into the social group and into the wider society in which the person finds him/herself. Defining affective and social health as social acceptability has some merit, especially if we consider the opposite extreme, where a person is completely cut-off from his/her surroundings and cannot communicate with other people. A socially isolated pupil is rightly a concern to teachers, and efforts need to be made to find out why that pupil is alone, to find them a group into which they might fit, and attempt to help them develop the social skills that will enable them to communicate and cooperate more easily with others. But, as we have seen, when we are assertive we respect ourselves too, and expect others to do the same. Encouraging appropriate sociability should not be mistaken for insisting on conformity, nor is making friends and fitting in with the group the be-all and end-all of mental health. If education is about empowerment and the pursuit of autonomy, it follows that social acceptability needs to be balanced with other considerations.

We have already discussed the need for schools to teach young people to think for themselves and be critical, independent thinkers. This process begins at the level of classroom and playground interaction, helping children and young people learn to accept and value their differences. Education for mental, emotional and social health includes learning to stick to the principles, beliefs and lifestyle we feel are right despite opposition, as long as to do so does not hurt us or anyone else, and to defend the rights of others to do the same. It includes accepting that we all have a right to be different, and recognising and supporting individuality, diversity, cultural richness, different ways of knowing and feeling, and a certain degree of eccentricity, in oneself and others.

Increasing understanding of mental illness

We have said that is helpful to see mental health and illness as a contin-uum, and to recognise that any of us could suffer from mental illness. But such a view is far from common, and there is an enormous fear of mental illness in others, and a consequent reluctance to admit it in oneself. Mental health and illness have always been surrounded by potent language and pejorative and distancing attitudes. As a result, people who have been labelled as mentally ill experience a great deal of prejudice, fear, misunder-standing and often some hatred. Pupils can be bullied, and teachers who have had a psychiatric or stress-related episode may well find it difficult to get a job in the future. There is a huge temptation for staff, pupils and their parents to play down such problems, to soldier on, or to give their condition another name rather than risk being labelled and stigmatised. The result is collusion: none of us understands the issue any better.

So a particular group in need of greater tolerance and understanding are those who have been labelled 'mentally ill', whether pupils or staff. We need to help people recognise too that this group is potentially very large, and might at some time include ourselves, and will certainly include our friends and relatives. Several recent projects in the UK have attempted to increase understanding of mental illness. For example, Mind have produced materials for secondary schools (Mind 1997) that help pupils examine their own attitudes to mental health through discussion, literature and film. Y Touring, who are the YMCA's national touring theatre company, recently toured schools with a play, 'Cracked', which examined and challenged perceptions of mental illness. Meridian Broadcasting have produced a pack to help young people understand and talk more effectively about mental health (Meridian Broadcasting Charitable Trust 1998).

Having examined some basic social competences, we look at how they can be applied to one of the most difficult problems that face schools – the management of conflict.

Managing conflict

Bullying

We have already quoted the worrying figures that demonstrate how widespread bullying is. Bullying is to be found in most schools, and most agencies and schools now take the problem very seriously: some ENHPS schools have made its prevention their main priority (HEA 1995b). There have been several excellent summaries of the best evidence on strategies that work to prevent bullying in schools (Rigby 1996; Tattum and Lane 1989; Olweus 1995), and the findings of such studies very much reinforce the messages that are put forward elsewhere in this book. For example, some of the principles that have emerged are that a long-term perspective is needed (Boulton and Flemington 1996); schools need to use a whole school approach that includes not only clear disciplinary policies and procedures but appropriate staff development, curriculum strategies and parental involvement (Arora 1994); the most helpful and preventive school ethos and environment are characterised by warmth and positive interest (Olweus 1995); and attempts to understand the perspective of both victim and bully are more helpful than exclusively punitive solutions (Robinson and Maines 1997). This book has very much drawn on such work on bullying in formulating its broader conclusions about the wider and more inclusive issue of promoting mental, emotional and social health, and so it is not necessary to go into detail about the issue of bullying separately: it is touched on implicitly and explicitly throughout. We will, however, look at a perspective on the problem of school violence and disruption that may be less familiar to European readers, that of conflict resolution, and explore the role that this approach can play in an overall strategy to reduce violence and discord in schools, and help everyone get along better.

Conflict is normal

Much work on conflict resolution comes from the US, where the need for it is particularly acute: the violence, gang fights and use of weaponry that has become a part of neighbourhood life for many children has now permeated schools, and in many of them children are now frisked on entry, and guards patrol the corridors. The occasional tragedies in which gun-toting pupils or ex-pupils shoot their colleagues and teachers, and not only in the US, remind us how vital it is that we find ways to help young people resolve conflicts in non violent ways, but they are only the newsworthy tip of the iceberg. Conflict is an everyday problem that faces most of us. Just as we all have a dark as well as a light side, so human relationships cannot be all sweetness and harmony: each of us has different needs and interests that need to be managed, and inevitably that creates interpersonal conflicts between people, conflicts that can then be managed positively to produce outcomes which move the situation on and create a greater understanding between participants. Growth comes about through the resolution of personal and social conflicts, not by ignoring them. So our social competences need to include the ability, not just to avoid conflict, but to resolve it when it occurs, to help others to do so, and to compromise, mediate and negotiate.

Conflict resolution programmes can be effective

Conflict resolution has proved to be a very fruitful concept for mental, emotional and social health education. Many schools, in the US and elsewhere, use conflict resolution as the organising framework for their programme of social and emotional education, sometimes linked with health promotion (Weiler and Dorman 1995). Reviews of such pro-grammes have concluded that they are on the whole useful (Powell, Muir Mcclain and Halasyamani 1995), but that there needs to be more evaluation of them (Weissberg and Elias 1993). Many programmes have strong links with local communities, and bring the community into the school as advisers (Giuliano 1994). Demonstrably effective programmes include the Resolving Conflict Creatively Programme in New York City public schools described by Lantieri and Patti (1996) in their evocatively named book, *Waging Peace in our Schools*. Another is the Positive Adolescents Choices Training (PACT) (Hammond and Yung 1991), a risk reduction programme developed in response to the need for violence prevention programming in Dayton, Ohio, targeted specifically at black adolescents. Conflict resolution has begun to be used in British schools too, for example, the Conflict and Change project in the London borough of Newham (Antidote 1998), and in Australia (Bretherton, Collins and Ferretti 1993).

The principles of conflict resolution

Conflict resolution is a concept that came originally from business in the twenties. It has many similarities with assertion theory, and is based on many of the competences already discussed, especially active listening, empathy and assertion. It confronts conflict rather than attempting to ignore or diffuse it, but non-violently. The essence of conflict resolution is that differences are resolved through helping participants to arrive at so-called 'win–win' outcomes, in which each party gets some of what they want. In conflict resolution the warring parties are encouraged to see the conflict as a problem to be solved, not an issue to be won. The goal is to promote caring and cooperative behaviour, and the vehicle is principled negotiation with a focus on issues, not personalities. Such conciliatory attitudes are highly useful ones to encourage in children and young people in attempting to resolve their everyday classroom and playground disputes, and are equally useful in highly charged staff-rooms.

Conflict resolution is most useful in inflammatory situations, where arguments threaten to get out of hand and risk at best broken relationships and at worst physical violence. The aim is to help pupils to devise ways to defuse the situation, often by taking action in a particular and predefined sequence, which help participants move down the escalator of negative feelings and which use a whole range of alternatives to violence. It may help to make the process more understandable to the reader to take a moment to work through the usual sequence. First, participants are encouraged and allowed to cool off, take deep breaths, and acknowledge their own feelings. The techniques of anger management outlined in Chapter 3 can help here. They then might talk about what happened, using active listening skills, and discuss how they got to feel that way. After that they go on to talk about what each wants out of the situation. The next and vital step is to agree to try to work it out together, share points of view on the subject, and really listen to the other person. They then may agree to disagree, to walk away, or more positively to take responsibility for finding a joint solution to problems. Finding a way through may involve first generating many possible solutions, then deciding together what the best one is and doing it. In a win/win situation the final outcome may be no one's first choice, but it may be the only one that all can live with.

Engaging in the development of such a logical and mutually agreed strategy reinforces in children and young people the empowering sense that they have choices about how they act, that there are different ways forward out of difficult situations, and that positive outcomes are possible. They teach the importance of avoiding conflict by practising the social competences of listening and cooperative skills, and avoiding insults and put-downs.

Mediation

Initially in conflict resolution it is the teacher who is called on to play the role of mediator, and indeed it is important that teachers know how to do it successfully. But adults as mediators have disadvantages: they inevitably bring with them the trappings of power and authority, which encourages pupils to be seen as in the right rather than to trying to find solutions. It is a time-consuming process that does little to empower children and young people to sort out their own problems when adults are not present.

Many schools have found that educating children and young people to act as mediators is a useful additional instrument in their efforts to reduce and resolve conflicts (Johnson *et al.* 1992; Benson and Benson 1993). Such pupils act as peacemakers, intervening in pupil conflicts without necessarily needing an adult, but knowing too when a situation is beyond their competence and when they need to ask for help. Using a pupil as mediator encourages participants to focus on the process and work the situation out for themselves. The solution is worked out by those in conflict: the mediator does not offer solutions, but asks questions using all the kinds of non-judgemental listening and responding skills we have already discussed.

In practice, the approach is again one of careful sequencing. When a conflict breaks out either the disputants themselves, or perhaps a concerned bystander, will call a mediator. The mediator arrives at the scene and offers their services. First, he or she attempts to get all parties to agree on ground rules, such as no violence, that each person be allowed to finish what they are saying, and that there be no verbal abuse. The disputants are each invited to give their side of the story, and then to discuss what happened, after which the mediator restates and summarises the stories until all agree on a version of reality. The disputants are then encouraged to brainstorm solutions, while the mediator moves back and forth between them helping them to focus on potential solutions. Finally, all find a form of words or action on which they can agree, accepting that such a solution will not be perfect for either party, but is a compromise with which they can live.

Mediation has been found to be very effective in producing a school atmosphere and ethos of non-violence and cooperation. Teachers report fewer fights, fewer verbal squabbles and much less time-consuming interventions for them (Lantieri and Patti 1996). Those who are not involved in the conflicts, but who in the past might have helped to inflame them, have a more positive role to be helpful and constructive. It provides young people with effective role models from their own generation to whom they can look up and see as 'cool'. The mediators themselves gain a good deal from it in terms of self-esteem, respect of their peers and improved relationships with their friends (Stacey and Robinson 1997).

Mediation schemes are to be found not only in the US, but in other countries, such as Scotland, New Zealand, Australia and Norway (Lawrence 1999), while the English ENHPS also produced some school-based projects that focused on this (HEA 1995b). Those who believe in conflict resolution and mediation have high hopes for its global significance, and suggest that creating 'peaceable classrooms' can be seen as the first step in reducing the level of conflict and violence in families, in communities, nationally and even between nations (Lantieri and Patti 1996). Certainly, the principles of conflict resolution are as applicable in situations of international tension as they are in resolving playground squabbles.

Conclusion

Throughout the last two chapters we have examined a broad range of emotional and social competences, and made some suggestions as to how schools might promote them. In citing evidence from some of the programmes and initiatives that have attempted to foster these competences we have inevitably touched on many that involve the taught curriculum. The next chapter will look at the issues involved in teaching and learning about mental, emotional and social health in more detail, and bring out some of the general principles that need to underlie work in this area.

5 Classroom and curriculum issues

Goals of this chapter

Teaching and learning have a central part to play in anchoring the whole process of promoting mental, emotional and social health in schools. The competences that underpin social and affective health need to be taught explicitly and systematically both to pupils and teachers. Otherwise, leaving essential but generic matters to chance is a sure recipe for them not happening at all, or in very piecemeal and ineffective ways. Earlier chapters have already made suggestions about how the school might promote the competences that are central to mental, emotional and social health. This chapter looks in more detail at ways in which social and affective competences can be taught to pupils and teachers, looking both at the general principles that need to underlie curriculum and professional development in this area, and the specific role of various parts of the school curriculum in making the generic competences meaningful and relevant. Again, to remind us that teachers are often on the receiving end of these processes, the term 'learner' will be used as well as 'pupil'.

Some key curriculum principles

Find out where people are starting from

We talked earlier of the need for schools to review where they are starting from before starting any programme of change. Similarly, we need to find out where our learners are starting from in terms of their knowledge, beliefs and feelings (Weare 1992). Of course, good teachers do this intuitively all the time through routine classroom talk and through reflecting on learners' work and progress. But there may well need to be a more systematic review of learners' competences, especially if it is to form the basis for any ongoing evaluation. Many schools have found ongoing reviews provide a useful basis for work, for example, some ENHPS schools in Poland regularly use questionnaires, interviews and focus groups to identify learner needs and expectations (WHO 1997b).

We have seen that listening and talking are central to the promotion of social and affective health, so including formal and informal interviews with individuals and groups must be the single, irreplaceable heart of any detailed and user-friendly programme for finding out where people are starting from. Through talk we can explore nuances and attitudes, find out what people are thinking, and help people to feel involved. However, talk is time consuming and unsystematic, and may not get to all learners, some of whom may be reluctant to talk about their beliefs and feelings.

Self-completion questionnaires are one of the most commonly used methods of data collection to inform programme development and evaluation. They provide very useful ways of gathering quantifiable information from lots of people quite quickly, and have the advantage of being anonymous, and thus encouraging frankness (Chapman *et al.* 1999). Many schools use questionnaires, sometimes developing their own instruments, sometimes using some of the published instruments that have been developed in universities and elsewhere. In the UK, the questionnaire developed by the University of Exeter (Balding 1998) is widely used, and includes valuable questions on self-esteem, anxiety and bullying. The Health Behaviour of School Age Children questionnaire (WHO 1999) has been used right across the world: the basic questionnaire includes questions on mood, and there is an optional package with ten questions on self-esteem.

However, questionnaires have limitations, especially in probing sensitive areas such as mental, emotional and social health. Their format can seem intimidating to learners, being reminiscent of an exam. The questions are pre-set, and may not be answered honestly, or may not get to the real issues or understandings of learners. They cannot be used with those too young or without the literacy skills to complete them. To overcome some of the weaknesses of questionnaires as a user-friendly mechanism, while retaining their ability to gather fairly objective data from a great many people quickly, a strong and original research strand has been developed using 'projective' methods (Oppenheim 1966), which is being used extensively within health education, including within the ENHPS (McWhirter and Wetton 1995). These methods involve asking learners to respond spontaneously, with writing and/or drawing, to an open-ended invitation, which can be completed in a whole range of ways and has no 'right answer'. Typical activities include 'bubble dialogue', filling in dialogue and/or thoughts in a bubble over the head of a cartoon figure, and/or completing an 'unfinished sentence'. Other widely used techniques include 'draw and write' (Wetton and McCoy 1998), which invites children to draw someone doing something, and then write about it, or tell the teacher what they want the teacher to write for them. The open-ended methods have proved to be particularly useful for uncovering aspects of mental, emotional and social health. For example, the ENHPS mental and emotional health project (Weare and Gray 1994) suggested that teachers could ask learners to fill in the dialogue between two cartoon young people who were discussing 'something that worries me'. The project also presented a 'draw and write' in which learners 'draw someone feeling good/not good about themselves, and draw round them all the things that are making them feel that way' (ibid.: 3.18).

Projective methods have several advantages over questionnaires. They can help young people express complex thoughts on sensitive and difficult issues: by reporting what they think 'someone else of your age' might think or do, learners do not have to incriminate or embarrass themselves. If well designed, the methods have the advantage of not 'putting ideas into people's heads'. Those that do not involve any or much writing are useful with younger pupils or those with literacy problems. They also help the teacher see how learners put their ideas together, and give insights into their different types of rationality. Finally, and most important of all, children and young people enjoy doing them.

Build from where the person is, in small steps

Once we know where people are starting from, we can use this information to construct a learning programme that builds from where they are in small steps, which is essential if our programme is to be developmentally sound. We have seen that learning is about the active construction of reality, and one universal strategy we all employ in trying to understand an experience is that of trying first to fit a new experience into whatever mental categories, ideas and theories we already possess (Gagne 1965). Even a new-born baby begins life with some basic instincts that enables them to judge all objects and experiences in simple terms like 'edible/not edible'. Through experience we find that the world does not quite fit our simple view, and our minds gradually evolve more complex and sophisticated categories to match the complexity of the experience as we perceive it. This basic process has been described by many different psychologists, each using slightly different terms. Piaget for example (Piaget and Inhelder 1958) named the twin process of 'assimilation' (attempting to fit experience into our previous categories) and 'accommodation' (creating new categories in the mind when these no longer fit our experience). People learn most effectively from 'nearly new' experiences, which are just a little more complex than any they have met before, so that they can both make sense of it and adapt a little mentally. If an experience is too unlike what someone knows already, they tend to be unable to recognise it at all, or they are frightened or overwhelmed by it. If it is too like what he/she knows already, they tend to be bored by it. So teachers need to structure the learning experience to pose a challenge that is just fractionally more difficult than those with which the learner is familiar, and progress from there in small and well-defined steps.

Encouraging increasing independence

One of the key ways in which teachers need to graduate and structure the experience is in terms of the degree of dependence and independence for which the learner is ready. We have suggested that a key goal for social and affective education is an independent and critical learner, but that the empowerment approach sees such autonomy realistically rather than idealistically, as an end point, something that people have to be helped to achieve rather than an innate feature with which they start out. The growth of autonomy is about gradually internalising a sense of inner structure, security and power that one has first experienced in the outside world. Initially, the child is completely dependent, and only gradually becomes capable of increasing independence, both physical and psychological. Wise carers, both parents and teachers, will see part of their task as encouraging the child or young person to become increasingly independent, and to internalise a sense of power, while continuing to provide a basic bedrock of stability on which the child can trust and to which they can return as needed. Winnicott (1974) describes the interim stages as 'relative dependency'. There is a delicate balance to be struck between clarity and autonomy, boundaries and freedom, dependence and independence. Teachers need to be gently pushing the learner towards ever greater independence, while providing a secure base for their explorations, a theme that will run through all effective programmes of social and affective education.

Empowering classroom methodologies

Developing autonomy is not something we only do in certain lessons, it is a goal for the entire curriculum. One key way in which it can be realised is through the methodologies of teaching and learning that we use in the classroom. Empowerment uses powerful and proactive educational methods, often based on experiential learning and on counselling techniques, to tackle the inner and outer forces that block the growth of personal autonomy. Activities include, for example, clarifying beliefs and values, reflecting on learners' emotions, practising assertiveness skills, and developing critical abilities (Anderson 1988; Tones 1986). Such approaches are highly active and participatory, involving group work, role-plays, games, simulations and structured discussion. Projects that attempt to develop mental and emotional health in schools have invariably used such active and participative methods (Mosley 1993; Weare and Gray 1994; Lantieri and Patti 1996; Elias et al. 1997). Again, there is good evidence for the value of this approach: Elias and Allen (1991) showed that discovery learning was more effective than normal programmes for helping pupils generalise their social and emotional learning.

Although younger children in particular need the consistency and security of a regular classroom routine, on the whole most of us respond better when varied methods of teaching and learning are used. There is strong evidence that approaches to social and emotional learning which use a range of methods are more effective than those with a more limited repertoire (DuPaul and Eckert 1994), and that the need to employ variety is particularly strong when teaching adolescents and adults (Greenhalgh 1994; Sotto 1994). Using a wide range of methods of teaching and learning helps people to generalise their learning by giving them a range of contexts in which to practice their competences. It also helps the teacher to construct a range of learning experiences that can meet the different learning styles that learners have, and helps learners themselves develop a wider repertoire of approaches to learning.

But using an empowerment approach is far more than the superficial encouragement of 'busy' classroom activity, it involves a shift in power and focus from the teacher to the learner, and from the teaching to the learning process (Sotto 1994). The teacher is no longer the sole arbiter but is instead a facilitator, involving learners in responsibility for learning, and for the creation of a positive classroom climate. There is evidence that such involvement is highly effective: Schaps, Lewis and Watson (1996) found that pupils demonstrably worked harder and had better results if they worked in classrooms where they had a greater say in planning and deciding both what they learnt and classroom rules about behaviour, while Fantuzzo et al. (1988) evaluated twenty-six studies that directly compared teacher-managed and pupil-managed interventions in mainstream education: they found that pupil-managed interventions were more effective. A highly successful project in a school in Norway not only used peer education, with fourth-grade pupils teaching the second grade, but allowed both sets of pupils to determine its content and style, with teachers keeping a low profile as facilitators and guides: teachers were astonished at how responsible and creative the pupils were (WHO 1997b).

Positive approaches

We have said that schools need to focus on positive not negative behaviours, attitudes and outcomes, and this very much applies to approaches to teaching and learning. Although some teachers continue to believe in the power of fear, there is overwhelming evidence that negative approaches, which attempt to use 'scare tactics' to frighten learners into a healthier lifestyle are not only ineffective, but are often counterproductive: they should thus be seen as not only pointless, but possibly very dangerous for schools to use (Liedekerken et al. 1990). At best, young people will probably block out horrific or gory images as the mind has a highly useful defence mechanism of forgetting such things quite quickly. Even worse, some young people find the suggestion that an activity is risky adds to its glamour. We know, for example, that many young people believe that they are themselves strong enough not to succumb to addiction to nicotine or heroin, and can see taking it as a challenge to their own sense of toughness, so to emphasise its dangers may only make its lure more fatally attractive. So, however morally gratifying it may feel, teachers should shy away from using negative messages, and should find ways to teach in more uplifting, intriguing or amusing ways.

Teach skills and behaviours

We have suggested that the behavioural approach, used on its own, is insufficient. However, if used within the overall context of an empowerment and experiential approach, the teaching of behavioural and cognitive skills most certainly forms a significant part of the picture. Evidence shows clearly that people are only likely to change their behaviour if they are exposed to extensive and explicit learning, for example, about problem-solving strategies, skills, routines and decision-making paths (Elias 1990; Grossman and Hughes 1992), and that approaches which take an organised and systematic approach to teaching social and emotional competences are often highly effective in changing the behaviour of young people (Durlak 1995; Durlak and Wells 1997; Zaragoza, Vaughan and McIntosh 1991). Research by Hawkins and Catalano (1992) showed that young people benefited greatly from a structured programme on what they called 'pro-social' skills that not only taught them the skills, but had teachers model them, give them clear feedback on their attempts to practise them and positive reinforcement for using them well. In contrast, approaches that do not include such explicit skills training, but that attempt to teach attitudes and values alone have been shown consistently not to be so effective (Fertman and Chubb 1992). A study that compared a range of different approaches to teaching social competences found that only specific skills training made any difference (Vaughan and Lancelotta 1990). Another study that directly compared groups taught via the traditional approach to drug education of 'just say no' with groups given a systematic and elaborate programme of specific drug-refusal techniques, which taught appropriate social skills and provided them with a rationale for each response, showed that only the second group exhibited significant gains in their ability to refuse drugs in follow-up situations (Jones *et al.* 1990). Skills have a physical as well as a mental component: relaxation has been shown to be effective in curbing anxiety in adolescent boys (Hains 1992), exercise has been shown to improve the behaviour of difficult boys (Yell 1988), while Henderson *et al.* (1992) showed increases in participants internal locus of control following a stress-reduction programme.

The importance of skills training has been shown time and again, across a broad range of cultures (Eitan, Amir and Rich 1992; Guttman 1994; Hon and Watkins 1995), and to be helpful from a very early age (McGinnis 1984; 1990). So any successful comprehensive programme on mental, emotional and social health must include extensive, routinised, regular and predictable work to develop specific skills across the curriculum, and reinforce these skills by pupils' real-life experience across the whole school. In recognition of this, the majority of work in schools on promoting social and affective competences has employed a skills-based approach. Indeed, many programmes are focused entirely on skills: for example, the work of the WHO global task force for mental health in schools is based on a systematic and comprehensive 'Life Skills' approach (WHO 1994) to teaching a broad range of social and affective skills, which the originators claim have proved to be as relevant in 'Nigeria as ... in Pakistan, Jamaica, Poland or Hungary' (Lee 1994: 206). Such approaches have been well-developed in the UK, particularly through the comprehensive teaching packages produced by TACADE (Moon 1996; TACADE 1996), which teach a range of social and affective skills.

Emotional and social skills will not be picked up by osmosis if they are left vague and implicit: only by regular rehearsal and practice of the component elements of skill will learners become emotionally and socially literate. Regular practice is particularly important if we consider that pupils will often come to the classroom having acquired some very dysfunctional skills and attitudes, such as aggressive or defensive responses when they feel threatened, which need to be replaced with more helpful responses. Unlearning is a process that is a good deal more difficult and time-consuming than learning something completely novel, yet schools often teach traditional subjects, which are mostly new to children, with all the system, resource and time allocation they can muster, while leaving the learning of emotional and social competences to chance.

Step-by-step approach

Given that childhood and, to some extent, adolescence are a time of concrete thinking, most pupils need grounded, easy, generic and stepwise strategies for solving their emotional and social problems. Adults can also find these approaches helpful. The stepwise problem-solving strategies that help pupils to solve personal and social problems encourage pupils to think through a problem in stages. These stages include getting clear what the problem is, identifying a range of alternative solutions, examining their pros and cons and their long and short-term implications before settling on one, and reflecting on the outcome as a guide to future action (Elias and Tobias 1996). We have already examined some problem-solving strategies that use specific steps and sequences when we looked at the processes involved in anger management in Chapter 3 and in conflict resolution in Chapter 4.

Stepwise 'thinking strategies' have been used by a huge number of projects, such as the Promoting Alternative Thinking Strategies Project (Paths) (Greenberg and Kusche 1993; Greenberg *et al*. 1995), and have been effective in helping adolescent boys with anxiety (Hains 1992). Teachers can use the more time-consuming but effective technique of 'scaffolding' or engaging pupils in a prolonged sequential dialogue in which the teacher carries out some of the task for the pupil so they can focus on problem solving, but in a highly structured, step-by-step manner (Elias *et al*. 1997): this can be done with individual pupils in difficulties or with a whole class.

To help pupils remember the steps easily, many emotional and social skills based programmes use acronyms, visual images and mnemonics as tangible prompts to remind pupils of simple step-by-step approaches to problem solving, and Goleman (1996) and Elias *et al*. (1997) describe several such approaches. A programme used in New Haven is a typical example: it uses the mnemonic SOCS, which encourages pupils to reflect on the Situation, review their Options, think of the possible Consequences, and then try what seems to be the best Solution (Elias *et al*. 1997). Other schemes use the visual reminder of 'traffic lights', such as the Australian 'stop–think–do' scheme, to give pupils a visual image to summarise the stages involved (Petersen 1992). Schools that use these techniques find it helpful to use the acronyms and visual 'cues' across the school, on notice boards and walls, to remind pupils and teachers to use the strategies in their normal activities.

Giving the learner control of the skills-based programme

One reason why many who believe in empowering approaches to learning dismiss the behavioural skills approach is that they see it as inevitably top down, teacher lead, de-powering and manipulative. Some have expressed concerns that coercing younger children into practising healthy behaviour may achieve short-term compliance, but risks a 'rebound' effect as children get older and more knowledgeable, and lose trust in the truthfulness of their teachers (Stewart-Brown 1998).

We have said, however, that work with adults has shown that a behavioural, skills-based approach can be used in ways that are voluntaristic and learner-centred. Skills-based behavioural approaches can be empowering to young people too if the management of them is put in the hands of the pupils themselves (Besalel-Azrin, Azrin and Armstrong 1977). Many programmes have developed concrete and structured strategies to help pupils to set their own self-management goals and monitor their own progress through self-reflection, using techniques such as self-assessment, self-recording and self-reinforcement (Nelson *et al*. 1991). Self-management programmes are most common in the US, but they have been used elsewhere: Ronen (1994) describes teaching a programme of self-management skills in Tel Aviv, Israel, in which second and sixth-grade pupils were taught self-control as part of their normal curricula, applied through classroom and home-based homework assignments. Computer-based software is also beginning to be developed to help pupils think through these processes (Elias and Tobias, 1996).

There is again considerable evidence for the effectiveness of self-management techniques. Ninness (1995) looked at a range of self-management programmes and concluded that they resulted in substantial improvement in pupils' use of social skills in natural situations, such as not responding to taunting in dinner queues, even when no adults were present, while Webber *et al.* (1993) looked at twenty-seven self-management studies and found that self-monitoring was very successful in increasing attention to task, positive classroom behaviours, and improving social skills. Morris (1982) found that asking the pupils to determine their own behavioural goals caused them to become more reflective about what events bring about certain behaviours, to be more observant, and improved their self-image.

Self-monitoring demonstrably has the additional benefit over traditional behaviour modification systems of enhancing the likelihood that positive classroom behaviours will generalise to other settings. Neilans and Israel (1981) compared the effectiveness of a self-regulation package, consisting of self-monitoring, goal-setting, evaluation and self-reinforcement with that of a traditional behaviourist token economy system. Although both systems resulted in significantly decreased disruptive behaviour and significantly increased on-task behaviour, the changes were greater and were maintained longer under the self-regulation system.

Generalising to real life

Empowerment tends to take a generic and process-oriented approach rather than a topic-based one. Traditionally, school health education has tended to concentrate on physical health issues, and on specific health topics, such as drug misuse, diet and exercise. However, the empowerment approach to health promotion sees behaviour that relates to physical health, and to specific issues such as smoking or sexual behaviour, as determined by deeper attitudes, such as self-esteem and empathy, and teaches generic competences such as self-esteem, communication, assertiveness and decision-making, rather than focusing on specific topics, imparting of information, or teaching isolated behaviours (Macdonald 1994).

It is important that the competences young people are taught are indeed sufficiently generic, and not just tied to specific situations. Programmes that attempt to teach basic, foundation competences appear to be more effective in changing young people's specific behaviour, for example, in preventing and/or reducing violence, aggression, bullying, truancy, school drop-out, teenage pregnancy and drug abuse than are programmes that isolate and concentrate on those specific behaviours (Caplan *et al.* 1992; Durlak 1995). Indeed, programmes that attempt to teach specific skills to avoid drug misuse, child abuse or sexual behaviour can backfire quite often and increase the problem they were supposed to prevent (Botvin and Dusenbury 1989).

A vital step in teaching competences is helping people to generalise from the specific situation in which they first learned the skills to real-life situations. The ability to generalise is difficult for all of us, and by no means comes naturally, especially to the young, whose patterns of thought are far more concrete than those of adults (Houghton 1991), while slower pupils find generalisation particularly difficult (Langone *et al.* 1995). Reviews of the success and failure of specific skills teaching show that many initiatives fail to have any wider or long-term impact because they do not help pupils to generalise their learning (Brigham 1989; Coleman *et al.* 1993; Beelmann *et al.* 1994; Hollin 1990). Conversely, approaches that explicitly teach the skills of generalisation, and help pupils practice in real-life situations, have been shown to be highly effective (Durlak *et al.* 1994).

The most useful way to teach people to generalise is to use their real-life experience as the medium for teaching (Houghton 1991). All of us, whatever our age, tend to learn more powerfully through real-life experience than through the intellect: indeed Rollinson (1992) suggests that this is the only learning that really counts in emotional and social education. So it is by no means enough to talk about feelings and emotional issues, we need the actual experience, for example, of working through an emotion, of personal accomplishment, of feeling valued and loved, of getting it right. This experience has to take place in everyday social interaction, in real time, if we are to believe in its significance and allow it to change our minds, our feelings, our behaviour. So, far more significant than the initial teaching of a skill is the follow-up coaching that takes place in real life. There is evidence, for example, that pupils learn social skills best in the company of people with whom they would typically establish relationships (Carey and Stoner 1994), and that social skills education is only effective if it has genuine consequences for pupils in the classroom (DuPaul and Eckert 1994). Teachers need to make considerable use of the experiences of their pupils, and encourage and foster the practising of real-life skills and routines. Discipline problems can be seen as a good opportunity to teach social and emotional skills if, instead of simply punishing, we focus on the logical consequences of actions and try to find positive solutions.

*Using the whole school as the context for practising
the competences*

In the process of skill acquisition, role modelling is particularly key. On the whole, pupils focus on what teachers do rather than what they say, and where they perceive a discrepancy are most likely to mimic what is modelled (Mize and Ladd 1990). So teachers themselves need to demonstrate the kind of respectful, tolerant, warm and supportive behaviour that they want pupils to exhibit, and look after their own mental, emotional and social health, not only on their own account, but so they can provide a positive example to their pupils.

Whatever approaches, programmes and schema are used, they need to be known by everyone in the school and practised across all lessons, and in the school as a whole. The everyday world of the school contains endless opportunities to practise competence building, for example, when pupils have to wait their turn in class or in the dinner queue, respond to bullying and taunting of themselves and others in the playground, are pressurised to smoke, feel anxious about how they will do in a forthcoming test or exam, or prepare to take a penalty on the playing field. Perceptive and well-prepared adults can take advantage of 'the golden moment' of a teaching opportunity that can occur spontaneously when circumstances have made the pupil especially ready to learn, and ensure that they provide the essential reminders and coaching. Once pupils have practised and applied the competences in controlled, adult-supervised situations, they then have the foundation from which to apply these skills outside in their everyday, routine interactions and to remind each other of them.

It is crucial too that the everyday emotional experiences that children have reinforce the messages we want them to learn. Feelings run deep and long, especially those about ourselves, and the attitudes pupils and teachers have, such as low self-esteem or a lack of belief in their power to change things, are usually based in reality as they have experienced it. The self concept is built very early from our initial experiences in the home, and reinforced by our later experiences in school and elsewhere. Replacing a negative self-image with a positive one is not achieved overnight by a bit of positive talking. There is more to changing people's beliefs than asking them to change or helping them practise the skills alone, although these can help: we need to make sure that their experience of their social world then endorses the changes we are trying to help them make. A person will need to have many concrete, positive experiences of feeling loved and valued before they begin to be able to value themselves. They will need time and help to understand why they feel as they do if they are not simply to repeat the patterns they have adopted as mental habits. For many children, such as the isolates, the misfits and the belligerent, helping them change will take considerable time, energy and planning.

Using whole class meetings and circle time

There is a general consensus among those who have practical experience of working in schools to promote mental, emotional and social health that regular class meetings and whole class discussion are essential to the process (Elias *et al.*, 1997; Lantieri and Patti, 1996; Wetton and Cansell, 1993). Such discussions give pupils a chance to practise many of the key competences, such as listening, being assertive, empathising and resolving conflicts, and the method has a vast range of applications. Used consistently, productive class discussion gives pupils a model they can work with when the teacher is not there, and helps them take the essential step of generalising to their everyday experience.

Productive and effective whole class discussions do not just happen; they demand considerable skill from the teacher in managing them in ways that encourage all to participate and feel safe in having their say, that ensure that all remain engaged and boredom does not set in, and which get the right balance between realism and positive thinking. If young people are to feel safe enough to speak, it is essential that there are 'ground rules' about confidentiality, listening to others without interruption, and avoiding sarcastic and negative 'put-downs'. In many classrooms that use whole class discussions extensively, one of the first events of the year is a whole class discussion of such ground rules for class behaviour, and pupils will themselves have a lot to say about getting the rules of class interaction straight (Elias and Tobias 1996). Pupils can also usefully be involved in formulating rules on classroom management, such as how they should ask for the teacher's attention and how the teacher should ask for quiet, how they should finish the lesson, and so on.

The importance of thinking about classroom seating during such discussions has been highlighted through the impact of circle time, a method that has become very influential in British primary schools. In circle time, discussions take place in a circle that includes the teacher, and this has a major influence over its powerful effectiveness in encouraging open discussion, sharing and cooperativeness (Wetton and Cansell 1993; Mosley 1993; 1996). Circle time is often highly structured, with each pupil being invited to speak without interruption on a particular topic, sometimes with the help of an object that is passed round. Those who do not want to contribute can simply 'pass'. Such structure encourages vocal pupils to wait their turn, and to stick to the theme rather than react impulsively to the previous statement, while providing quieter pupils with a safe and protected opportunity to speak. Exponents of circle time see it as a highly powerful method, which has a key place in teaching mental, emotional and social health, and in building empathy, respect and a sense of mutual support in the whole school community.

Teachers who spend time on such apparently 'non-academic activities' at the beginning of the year actually find they have more time later for academic ones, as the activities help pupils begin to manage their potentially disruptive emotions, and set a tone of positive cooperation. Classes are more likely to run smoothly, pupils are more likely to be more involved in their own learning, and a greater number of pupils are more likely to participate. Over time, as such practices become routinised, schools find that they spend more time on productive activity and waste less time dealing with unresolved conflicts and behavioural and emotional problems (Elias *et al.* 1997). Classrooms that schedule in such whole class discussions regularly find that they lead to better behaviour and less strife, as children often save their problems for whole class discussion rather than reacting to them immediately (Lantieri and Patti 1996).

Cooperative group work

We have remarked that many who work in this field see schools as a key institution in promoting social and even global values of peacefulness, cooperation and responsible citizenship (Hawkins and Catalano 1992; Brahma Kumaris, 1995; Kessler, 1997). We have made much of the need to learn social competences, which help young people develop from the egocentric world of the child into the more cooperative world of the adult. McCallum and Bracken (1993) suggest that healthy relationships are characterised by mutually reinforcing exchanges that lead to socially desirable consequences, and that cooperative learning environments offer the greatest promise to educators for promoting such healthy relationships among pupils.

But young people are unable to become more cooperative in classrooms where learning is always individualised and where competition is always the norm. So there is a need to reward cooperation as well as competition (Johnson and Johnson 1992; 1994) and to give pupils tasks for which they are jointly responsible at least some of the time. A recent global project has developed approaches and materials for teachers to use to promote cooperation (Church *et al.* 1990). Well-planned cooperative work in small groups has an essential part to play in developing emotional and social competences, such as empathy, listening, sensitivity, negotiation, conflict resolution and cooperation. It tends naturally to lead to an increase in the 'fun' level in the classroom, which can be encouraged through the use of games, which can increase a sense of group solidarity through shared laughter, and give a sense of group responsibility for keeping the game going. Group work also has a more generic part to play in more general cognitive and academic development, and group learning has been shown to be more effective than individual learning in encouraging problem solving through generating possible solutions, and jointly deciding on the best outcome (Nastasi and Clements 1991).

There is a wealth of evidence for the effectiveness of well-run group work on social and emotional competences. William Kreidler (1984), who invented the phrase 'the peaceable classroom' in the 1970s, saw his main educational goal as teaching his primary school class the skills of cooperation. He employed six basic principles, which were cooperation, caring communication, the appreciation of diversity, the appropriate expression of feelings, responsible decision-making and conflict resolution, and found, as he developed his use of group work, that the children's work and the classroom atmosphere improved drastically (Powell 1993). Cooperative group work has been found to be effective in teaching pupils social skills and cooperation (Morton 1993), and where it has been compared with work in conventional classrooms it has been found to be far more effective in teaching interpersonal skills (Farivar 1991). Group work has proved to be particularly useful for those with special needs. For example, Salend and Sonnenschein (1989) examined the effectiveness of a cooperative learning strategy on the behaviours of emotionally disturbed adolescents: they found that a cooperative learning strategy led to an increase in the classes' on-task, cooperative and academic behaviours – effects that were maintained over time. Group work has been used successfully to teach social skills to friendless children (Rosenthal 1993). Marchant (1995) found that using problem-solving activities that demanded collaboration and mutual self-help with a group of young children with emotional and behaviour difficulties taught them to live together without the constant aggression and hostility that had marked their previous interactions.

There is a great deal more to producing an effective group than just putting people together. Unfortunately, few teacher education courses teach the skills of running groups effectively or understanding group dynamics, which is a shame as such skills are very empowering to teachers. It is helpful to understand the way in which groups perform, and the stages that groups go through as they grow and change, with members moving from being isolated individuals competing with each other to, if the group is working well, being a coherent group, which gives support, in which people are able to be open and trusting (Stanford 1995). Like whole class discussion, group work does not just happen; it has to be carefully planned and sequenced. Pupils very much have to learn the skills of cooperation as they do not come naturally to egocentric youngsters. Individual pupils need to have reached a certain level of social competence before they can cooperate, with basic skills in self-control, the ability to take turns and group roles, and some basic abilities in communication. Such competences have been shown to be teachable to very small children through play (Ferrentino 1990). The task too has to be right, being one in which pupils realise that they can achieve more together than they can apart. There needs to be plenty of time set aside for the group to reflect on and evaluate the process of working in a group and their own role within it (Lantieri and Patti 1996).

Group work also has a central part to play in staff development. Working in individual classrooms can be very isolating, and staff too need to learn to work together as a team, recognising that they each have different roles to play, and valuing the contribution that different types of team members can bring to the overall process.

Peer education

We remarked in Chapter 2 that the peer group is the most powerful social influence on most adolescents, and that teachers need to use it, not fight it. Peer education, in which learners teach each other, has been shown to have a dynamic part to play in social and affective education. Lowenstein (1989) suggests that using peer groups can have a powerful influence on individual members, and can be used to bring about change in negative behaviour patterns by confronting young people with the results of their behaviour, creating a sense of shared decision-making and responsibility between young people and those who care for them, and finding alternatives to negative patterns, such as substance abuse. Peer tutoring can be used to promote academic learning too, while continuing to have a beneficial effect on young people's social and emotional competences (Franca *et al.* 1990). Peers do not have to be the same age as cross-age tutoring has been shown to be effective (Cochran *et al.* 1993; Maher 1982).

To take some well-evaluated examples, a study by Roswal (1995) found that pupils who worked in a collaborative peer tutor teaching programme demonstrated significant improvement in drop-out scores compared with pupils in both a traditional class using group learning and a traditional class using individual learning activities. Kaye and Webb (1996) found that a secondary school programme, which gave peer support to ease the transition from primary to secondary school, in which pupils from Year-six worked with small groups of Year-one pupils running a social education period for them once a week, was very positively evaluated by both groups of pupils. Using peers as counsellors can be particularly effective (Kim *et al.* 1992), and peer counsellors have been found to be as useful as professionals in reducing aggression in adolescent boys (Huey and Rank 1984).

Peer tutoring has proved to be particularly useful for difficult pupils, and behaviourally disturbed young people can themselves be very effective social and emotional educators (Gable, Arllen and Hendrickson 1994). Scruggs, Mastropieri and Richter (1985) reviewed seventeen studies that used tutoring interventions involving behaviourally and/or emotionally disturbed children: their results suggest that tutoring with behaviourally disturbed pupils has a positive effect on the academic functioning and attitude to academic work of both the tutee and the peer tutor, while improving the social relationship between them. In another study, a group of aggressive and withdrawn pupils were given a five-week programme of peer tutoring, after which they had higher self-concepts, made greater behavioural improvements, and demonstrated renewed interest in school and in the learning process compared with a control group (Lazerson 1980). Adolescents with learning and behaviour problems who served as peer tutors in a behavioural programme, giving reinforcement to other pupils for on-task behaviours were both effective at doing this as far as other pupils were concerned and themselves made academic and social gains in their own behaviours, which generalised to their behaviour across the school as a whole (Polirstok 1986).

Peer education can help integrate young people with special needs into the mainstream classroom. Goodman, Powell and Burke (1989) discussed the implementation of the 'buddy system', an intervention strategy implemented in a large urban school district to improve the behaviour of learning disabled children in the regular classroom. Pupils were taught to observe, monitor and reinforce appropriate behaviour exhibited by peers, and this awareness assisted pupils in controlling their own behaviours. They concluded that the buddy system was highly effective in helping learning disabled youngsters behave in ways that enabled them to stay in normal classrooms.

Having explored some of the key curriculum principles in this area, we look now at the part that some of the subjects that schools are already teaching can play in helping to deliver a comprehensive, systematic and planned teaching strategy for the promotion of mental, emotional and social health.

Teaching through school subjects

Health, personal and social education

Many schools in the UK teach some variation on health, personal and social education, while some European schools are developing health education curricula, so this forms one of the most obvious contexts for the teaching of social and affective competences.

As we have suggested in Chapter 1, health education has changed radically over the last decade or so, and in many contexts has moved on from its earlier focus on physical health, teaching isolated health topics, and the simple imparting of information. Health education, or at least that which is in the forefront of the discipline, now tends to employ a broader generic approach, which looks at mental as well as physical health, and which works on the underlying skills and attitudes that govern health behaviour, such as self-esteem, making choices and resisting pressure. It is thus often combined with personal and social education, and the three can become indivisible (Ryder and Campbell 1988).

There are now a number of broad-ranging health education curriculum programmes that take such a holistic and process-oriented approach, and several of them contain specific work on teaching many of the competences that help promote mental, emotional and social health. For example, the health education project most used in primary schools in the UK, Health for Life, devotes one-third of its content to 'relationships'. In Europe, the manual *Promoting the Health of Young People in Europe*, produced by the ENHPS, which is used by teachers throughout Europe (Metcalfe *et al.* 1993) devotes one-fifth of its contents to 'relationships and self-esteem' and 'assertiveness'.

We have said that young people need to learn to apply generic competences to specific instances, and so generic work on mental, emotional and social health needs to be supported by work on specific health topics such as sexuality, HIV/AIDS, drugs, tobacco and alcohol. Such applied perspectives can help young people see the relevance of their learning in relation to particular issues, contexts and situations. Again, a common thread can run through such work on issues such as self-esteem, self-respect, self-protection, resisting pressure, decision-making, stress management, communication skills, negotiation, and so on (Adams 1998). We will now explore two of the most obvious arenas for work on mental, social and emotional health, namely sex education and drug education.

Health topics: sex education

Recent approaches to sex education have moved on from the traditional, narrow approach of concentrating on 'the plumbing', and the body in general as a discrete object, and on the negative issues of contraception and sexually transmitted disease. More modern approaches are now likely to start from a concern with more positive aspects of sexuality and with relationships as a context for its expression. The emphasis is increasingly on such holistic issues as loving and caring, looking after yourself and others, growing and changing, making decisions, taking responsibility, communicating effectively about wants and needs, being assertive and negotiating safer sex (Clarity Collective 1988; HEA 1989; Sanders and Swinden 1990). Some ENHPS schools have developed whole school programmes on sex education, which use competency-based approaches (HEA 1995b). This more social and affective approach to sex education then clearly provides one very obvious arena in which emotional and social competences can be developed.

Drug education

There has long been a strong link between social and affective education and drug education. Many programmes that attempt to promote mental, emotional and social health have grown out of concerns about drug use and are intended to tackle this problem (Jones *et al.* 1990; Hawkins and Catalano 1992). Drug education is nowadays often part of the curriculum not just of secondary schools, but increasingly of primary schools too, as research has shown that children are exposed to and have a complex understanding of drugs at a surprisingly early age (Williams *et al.* 1992b). So the drug education curriculum is proving to be another obvious opportunity to explore social and affective competences.

Recent published programmes in drug education generally go well beyond the simplistic imparting of information about drugs and their harmful effects and the 'just say no' approach of earlier times to look at underlying process issues, particularly decision-making, communicating effectively and resisting pressure. To take one example, the widely used Skills for Adolescence (TACADE 1996) is a drug-prevention programme designed specifically for young adolescents. It involves pupils in reading, writing, analysing and organising ideas, thinking critically and communicating with others in relation to the issue of drug use and abuse, and is designed to be used in a wide variety of lessons, including language, arts, social studies and health education. Evaluations have shown that the programme demonstrably increases self-confidence and the coping skills of participants, and helps participants to achieve a greater sense of having control of their lives (Ketchel and Bieger 1989). This project is a fairly typical one, and there are many other examples. In Ireland, for instance, a major primary prevention project aimed at drug abuse has based its activities on the themes of self-esteem, assertiveness, feelings and decision-making (WHO 1997b), while a Scottish drug and alcohol initiative has used a health promoting school approach (Coggans and McKellar 1995).

Goleman (1996) suggests that the root cause of dependence on drugs is an emotional one, with drugs and alcohol often being used to soothe feelings of anxiety, anger or depression. He cites evidence that those who report high levels of emotional distress are most likely to go on to be drug abusers. So one of the aims of teaching about mental, emotional and social health is most certainly to help people do away with, or reduce their need for, mood-altering drugs, including alcohol, tobacco and prescription drugs. If we can help people to have higher self-esteem, they may not need to use drugs to bolster their confidence; if they feel happier and more at ease, they may not need to use them to improve their mood; if they are more engaged in outgoing activities, they may not take them out of boredom; and if they are more assertive, they may feel able to resist pressures to take them from the peer group. All these are worthy and realistic goals to have for some of the people, some of the time.

It is also important to be realistic about what we can achieve with drug education, and to keep the issue in perspective rather than setting up the kind of moral panic that may alienate us from our pupils (Stears *et al.* 1995). We have to accept that taking drugs, including illegal substances, may well be harmful, but it is to some extent 'normal' in the sense that it is a very common practice among the young, including ordinary, well-adjusted, high achieving youngsters (HEA 1999). We might bear in mind that some kind of mind-altering substances have been used by humankind throughout history, and that most societies have a category of 'socially acceptable' drugs, which may themselves be very powerful and dependence inducing, such as alcohol and caffeine (Tudge 1998). Most societies have witnessed a massive rise in the taking of mood-altering prescription drugs, such as anti-depressants and tranquillisers, including in the adult population. Young people are very quick to spot hypocrisy, and do not appreciate being preached at by those who use drugs that they may consider just as harmful as their own preferred substances.

Some consensus on what makes school-based drug education effective is starting to emerge through some large-scale reviews of the evidence (Ives and Clements 1996; Tobler and Stratton 1997). Such reviews have shown, for example, that if schools wish to get involved in drug education they need to bear in mind that young people are often very knowledgeable about drugs, and that teachers themselves need to be knowledgeable about this issue before they teach it, or they risk being dismissed by their pupils as naive. Ill-informed drug education can do more harm than good: by overstating the dangers of drug use or suggesting that dependency is inevitable and absolute we may unwittingly add to the glamour that drugs have for some young people, and bolster the fatalistic myth that once harder drugs are used there is no way back. Of course, we must be well-informed about the risks of drugs, but we also need to recognise that most young people who experiment with drugs do not become permanently harmed or addicted. It may well be that we have to conclude pragmatically that we will never succeed in preventing all our pupils, or indeed all our teachers, from trying drugs, nor prevent a proportion of them from going on to use them.

Our goals must be broad and realistic if we are to be of serious help on the issue of drug use. For example, we need to include alcohol and tobacco in our concerns. This will then involve looking at school policies on these matters, and at teachers' own behaviours: we may, for example, need to think about what messages we are actually giving young people if the staff-room is a cloud of smoke or staff come back from the pub at lunch-time on a Friday smelling of beer. When we consider the taking of illegal drugs, we may need to aim at harm reduction (Lenton and Midford 1996), helping users to be aware of and avoid some specific and avoidable hazards in drug taking, rather than behaving as if they simply will not take them at all. Other realistic goals include helping people minimise their use, and supporting them in their attempts to give up. The school also has a role in helping parents with their own concerns about drug education, and assisting the friends and families of those who are the casualties of drugs cope with their reactions and feelings (Daw and Joyce 1996).

The evidence further suggests that it is best not to treat drug education as 'special', and certainly not to pass the buck by leaving it to be the subject of 'talks' by outsiders with an axe to grind, such as the police. Such one-off, isolated approaches may well do more harm than good by making drugs more sensational and thus more glamorous, but without being comprehensive enough to provide any serious assistance to help young people develop the competences they need to deal with them. Outside experts can have a role, but are best used to provide a specialised input as part of a wider, teacher-lead course, or to help plan a curriculum. As with all the issues that are concerned with mental, emotional and social health, drug education should be built into the curriculum in a natural, non-sensationalising, low-key, ongoing and spiral manner.

Teaching about mental, emotional and social health through traditional subjects

The next sections make suggestions about ways in which some traditional school subjects are related to mental, emotional and social health. It does not claim to be exhaustive, merely to provide some triggers for helping readers start to think through the links. These suggestions will by no means be novel as most teachers will, on reflection, realise that they are already touching on social and affective themes in their work. What may be new is the suggestion that such work can be more than opportunistic and haphazard, but can become a planned and sequential part of the social and emotional curriculum across the whole school, without any loss to the academic rigour of the subject in question.

Social and affective competences can be taught through any subject, often through its content, and always through its process. To take what is perhaps the least likely example, mathematics has been used successfully as the context for improving group cooperation (Farivar 1991), peer tutoring (Franca et al. 1990) and self-monitoring and self-management programmes (Kern et al. 1994).

We have already suggested that social and affective education should be seen as supporting the academic curriculum, not as in competition with it. Social and emotional learning is directly useful in helping pupils behave appropriately and think more clearly, whatever the subjects in question. Indeed, Maag (1990) suggests that distinctions between academic and social behaviour are arbitrary and unhelpful to both types of learning. The social and emotional competences are at root generic, and just as useful for academic subjects. For example, the basic skill of listening actively to what is said rather than what we think is being said is a vital part of being able to respond to the teacher's instructions. The stepwise problem-solving strategies that help pupils to solve personal and social problems are a generic cognitive process that is basic to any problem-based subject, especially the natural and social sciences (Hull 1987; Elias and Tobias 1996). Cooperative group work has been shown to benefit cognitive development and academic achievement as well as social and emotional learning (Nastasi and Clements 1991). Elias et al. (1997), who have done considerable work helping schools to develop whole school approaches, report that over time teaching emotional and social competences can become a seamless part of teaching, expressed through all that is said and done in the classroom.

The expressive arts

In the hands of some teachers, and under the influence of highly prescriptive national curricula and the need to engage in standardised assessment, the study of the arts can become a purely technical subject, concerned with the development of critical skills and technique. But to use this rather dry approach on its own is to remove much of the interest and point of the study of the arts, as well as to let slip a golden opportunity to use the arts to promote emotional and social development (Trelawney-Ross 1998; Department of Education and Science 1989). The expressive arts, such as literature, music, art, dance and drama are central to the development of mental, emotional and social competences (Greenhalgh 1994). The arts can give us powerful direct experience of a wide range of emotions, such as joy, excitement, tension and release, concern, fear, sorrow, and so on. Such experience can uplift us, expand and refine our emotional range. They can provide a highly pleasurable emotional experience through being, as the Greeks knew, cathartic, creating and then discharging complex and intense emotions. Such a joint experience can also be a powerful way to bring people together to create a sense of social solidarity (Kane 1994).

Music, for example, provides a valuable means of expression of direct emotion. It can be used in classrooms as a very powerful mood enhancer, to set the tone, start and close lessons, or as a starting point for writing or for discussion. Dance can liberate us from the constraints of language, help us express feelings and moods non-verbally, get in touch with our bodies and what they are telling us, and let off steam in a powerful and positive way. Fine art provides an opportunity for the direct self-expression of the emotions through form, shape, texture and colour, and an opportunity to explore how artists have used painting and other media for the expression of feelings. Pictures can also be used to help pupils improve their awareness of the significance of different facial expressions, and thus improve their social skills (Ekman *et al.* 1972).

There are several examples of the use of a range of expressive arts to teach emotional and social competences. Roberts (1997) describes a project where expressive activities, such as story, myth and tasks were used successfully to improve the behaviour of pupils with emotional and behavioural needs, including those who had suffered trauma. Kalliopuska and Tiitinen (1991) used role-play, story telling and music to increase both empathy and general sociability in adolescents, while Walsh (1990) describes a creative arts program in social skills training for early adolescents.

We will look now at an aspect of the arts that has a great deal of potential impact in this area – that of story telling.

Story telling: literature and the media

Story telling has a major role in developing mental, emotional and social health (Hunter, Phillips and Wetton 1998). Although the traditional medium for story telling in schools is the study of 'good' literature and the writing of 'the essay', television, film and video can be used, too, to bring the real world and its dilemmas into the classroom, and may have the advantage of being more immediately familiar to less literate pupils. Most stories, whatever their medium, are centrally concerned with the emotions and with relationships, and are thus one of the richest sources of material for promoting greater awareness and understanding of both the lighter and dark side of humanity, motivation, character and human dilemmas (Benninga and Belli 1982).

Stories are an ideal medium to use to promote empathy and understanding for others. For example, children and young people can be invited to retell a story from the point of view of various characters within it (Lantieri and Patti 1996). They can ponder how and why people did what they did, whether it is like or unlike their own experience, think of alternative ways forward for characters, how they could have got themselves out of conflicts and problems, and so on. Stories expand pupils' emotional horizons, proving a starting point for a discussion of feelings, dilemmas and situations that may be new or difficult for them. They help young people to cope with the challenges of life through anticipation, rehearsal and vicarious experience. Through stories, the young can experience some of the challenges of growing up, coping with fear, uncertainty, ambiguity, facing the future, coping with change, loss and disappointments in a safe context. They can be inspired by positive examples of honesty, bravery, loyalty, commitment and love. Stories that engage with the kind of problems children face also can help when children are going through a particular trauma, such as the divorce of their parents, illness, loss and bereavement or domestic violence by normalising and destigmatising the experience so they do not feel so isolated and odd (Geldard and Geldard 1997).

Of course, many teachers use literature and stories in this way, but often incidentally, as a footnote to their main concern with literacy and oracy, and without focusing pupils' attention on emotional and social matters in a planned manner. But, if used consciously, developmentally, and systematically, the results of using stories and pupils' own writing on their emotional and social development can be direct and dramatic. Jones (1994) reports a study in which pupils participated in ten weeks of instruction, including reading literature, discussion, journal writing and group projects around social and affective themes. Pupils learned better ways of resolving conflicts, were more honest in their assessments of situations, exhibited less careless behaviour, and complimented each other more instead of criticising.

Language

Chapter 3 suggested that emotional and social development is essentially concerned with language and its development, and that language has a key role to play in educating the emotions. Pupils can be encouraged to develop an emotional vocabulary to identify, name and distinguish feelings and affective states as part of their everyday language work (Greenberg and Snell 1997). The development of the ability to communicate is a vital part of feeling good about yourself and relating effectively to others (Farley 1987). Through creative writing, children can be encouraged to make up their own stories which can, again, increase their sense of mastery through putting their own emotions and experiences into words, and expand their ability to empathise through writing about the imagined experience of others.

Language is of course a potentially sensitive area, and can become a block to effective communication between the child and the school, or a source of self-esteem problems. We discussed the problem of educational underachievement at some length in Chapter 2, and language barriers can, if we are not careful, contribute to it. There are, for example, pupils for whom the language of the school is a second language, and those who do not speak 'standard English' in their home. Such pupils may come to feel inadequate, abnormal or alienated from the culture of the school. So, there is a need for schools in general, and language teachers in particular, to value the language children bring from home, and understand the language they use on the streets, as a way of bringing the school more closely together with the homes and the communities from which children come.

Drama and role-play

Drama is one of the most direct and vivid mediums for developing mental, emotional and social health competences, and has been used in a wide variety of ways. Some projects that attempt to promote health in general, and emotional and social health in particular, use improvised drama to provide triggers for audience activity (Women in Theatre 1996). This can involve acting a playlet in front of an audience, and then inviting them to discuss what has happened, to react, to suggest alternative ways forward that they then perform, and so on. Such activities can provide the audience with a powerful reminder of real life, give them a sense of involvement and their own potential power to change things, as well as reinforcing the idea that there are many possible outcomes to difficult situations, which can itself be very liberating.

The performing of scripted plays by the pupils themselves can help build self-esteem and confidence: like story telling it gets children used to expressing themselves through the words of other people, which assists in building empathy through understanding the world from another's point of view, especially if the teacher does not typecast but encourages them to take turns, and then reflect on their experience of being quite a different person for a while. Writing and acting their own plays, playlets and scenarios gives pupils even more power to literally 'write the script' for other people, to put themselves into the mind of a character and explore the dilemmas and challenges that face them. If such work is carried out in a group, it can be very influential too over the levels of pupil cooperation.

Improvised role-plays are a very powerful medium indeed for teaching a wide range of social and emotional competences, and have been used in a wide variety of projects. Some have employed this medium to teach assertion (Buell and Snyder 1981), conflict resolution (Tierney 1993), anger management (Kellner and Tutin 1995), the reduction of bullying (Foltz-Gray 1996), and to ease transitions for younger adolescents (Walsh-Bowers 1992). To take just two instances, Jupp and Griffiths (1990), in an Australian study, showed that shy and socially isolated adolescents who were taught through role-play became a good deal less shy, not only than those given no help, but those who experienced a more traditional discussion-based approach, while Frederickson and Simms (1990) showed that role-play can be very effective in improving social and emotional competences, including reducing aggression.

Role-play is clearly one of the most popular and powerful techniques on offer because of the valuable opportunity it provides to practice real-life skills in a safe environment, as many times as is necessary, and with feedback from others. Through role-play students can, for example, practise answering 'put-downs', giving strong messages, rehearsing solutions, expressing their feelings safely, and tackling prejudiced and racist behaviour. Role-play gives the opportunity to learn not only the words but the appropriate tone, body language and facial expressions to become more socially effective. It also improves the player's ability to read non-verbal and verbal expression in others. The scenarios can be teacher-initiated initially, but as they get used to it, the pupils can provide the scenarios themselves to see how problems or situations that bother them can be acted out and solved in different ways (Benninga and Belli 1982).

Like whole group discussion and small group work, organising success-ful role-play is not as easy as it looks: many adults and some pupils report that they dislike it, having had some poor experiences of the technique. Role-play needs to be run with considerable care and skill if all involved are to participate equally, feel adequately safe to take risks, and recognise and internalise the skills it is trying to teach. In particular, feedback on skills rehearsal must be given with caution and sensitivity. The 'rules' that have been evolved for giving feedback (Weare and Gray 1994) are simple but useful ones. These rules insist that: all involved must comment on the positives, in other words on what was done well, before going on to look at what could have been done better; the learner must go first and comment on his/her own performance before anyone else has a go; and all involved must use 'prescription not criticism', in other words saying positively what the learner might have done 'differently' rather than phrasing it in terms of what they have done 'badly'.

Physical education

We have said that mental, emotional and social literacy is based on bodily awareness, in other words the ability to 'read' what your body is telling you, that bodily language is a more powerful medium than oral language for conveying meaning, and that exercise is important for happiness and mental health (Barr 1985). Thus physical education, which recognises the importance of the body as well as the mind, can have a key role to play in the promotion of mental, emotional and social health. Physical education can provide an opportunity to improve self-esteem, particularly for pupils who are better at the physical than the intellectual side of the curriculum, and give a sense of mastery. Provided the competitive ethos is not allowed to become too dominant, physical education can teach the value of cooperation, teamwork and joint responsibility, and promote high standards of behaviour (Thomas 1993; Elias et al. 1997).

Some projects have made use of bodily activity specifically to promote emotional and social competences. Yell (1988) showed that behaviourally disordered pupils improved their behaviour as a result of thirty-minute jogging and exercise sessions, while Bender (1987) showed that young people can benefit greatly from being taught specific physical relaxation and stress-reduction techniques.

Biology

As our emotions are inextricably linked with our bodily reactions, so the study of biology has a good deal to contribute to the study of emotional and mental health. Pupils may find it very empowering to become more aware of the physiological basis of their emotional life, which may give them greater insight into their own reactions and help them to manage their own emotions more easily. They may enjoy examining what the emotions do to the body, and learning to recognise their own emotions, such as anger, fear, joy and stress, through their bodily reactions, such as raised heartbeat, flushing, sweating and churning stomach. There has been a good deal of fascinating recent work on the brain and emotion (Damasio 1994; Goleman 1996) that throws light on the problem of impulsivity and why new experiences can trigger powerful reactions based on previous

experiences, which pupils may find very useful in understanding themselves better.

Recent work on animal behaviour is also coming to emphasise the
importance of emotion: animals are increasingly no longer viewed as
insensate beings or bundles of mindless instincts, but as creatures with
complex emotions that are often very like our own. Studies of the role of
emotion in animal behaviour, for example, in survival, in self-preservation,
in reproduction and in social bonding, and the examination of the
similarities and differences between animals and humans, can provide a
way into this topic, which is likely to have great appeal to children and
young people, who generally find animals fascinating.

History

Traditionally, teachers approached history as if it was a series of facts and
dates, but the study of history has changed a good deal in recent years, and
some of its current goals bring it into an interesting and potentially
productive relationship with mental, emotional and social health
education. The goals of history teaching now include providing an
opportunity to broaden young people's horizons by encouraging them to
empathise with people who lived in the past, and think about the problems
they faced and how they solved them, goals that have a clear and direct
link to social and emotional competences. Others use the study of history
to teach the ability to sift evidence critically, and Elias *et al.* (1997) suggest
that the kind of step-by-step problem-solving approach we are encouraging young people to use in social and affective learning can generalise to
the skills of critical appraisal.

Pupils can be encouraged to think of the extent to which the understanding of history is a matter of understanding mass, and sometimes
individual, emotion, and how emotions are one of the triggers that drive
people, individually or collectively, to make a difference to the world, for
good or ill. They can examine ways in which emotions such as greed, fear,
territoriality, identification with an ethnic or religious group, tribe or
nation have lead to some of the terrible events of history, such as
invasions, wars and holocausts. They can also examine how more positive
emotions, such as a desire for peace, justice or humanitarianism, have lead
people to attempt to improve social conditions, to free oppressed people or
to find a solution to conflict. They may consider how the movers and
shakers of history, then and now, have usually seen themselves as acting
for the best of reasons, and how terrible outcomes may follow processes
set in motion for what the instigators saw as perfectly acceptable reasons
at the time. So the study of history can provide us with a valuable
opportunity to examine and understand the complex emotions that
motivate people, which in turn can tell us more about ourselves and our
own potentiality for good, for evil and for rationalisation.

Teacher education

Teachers need social and affective education too

This book has argued throughout that the need to learn social and affective competences is not just for pupils: it is, if anything, more vital that teachers learn them if they are to work with pupils effectively, change their school context, and be more fulfilled themselves. This final section will make a few concluding comments on the issue of teacher education.

Greenhalgh (1994) reminds us that in working with children and young people, teachers own emotions are necessarily involved: for good or ill, teachers react to the emotions and the behaviours of the pupils with whom they work. Unfortunately, as Lantieri and Patti (1996), who have extensive experience of teaching conflict resolution in schools, point out, one major difference between this area, and more traditional school subjects is that it is one in which teachers may well not be much further on than their pupils. Given the lack of basic education in this area, it is likely that teachers will have had little or no education on it themselves, unless they have been lucky or have sought it out. Emotional competence does not necessarily increase drastically with age, and it is a basic tenet of psychotherapy that many adults are simply larger versions of the child they once were, dominated by the same feelings and needs, perhaps better disguised, but no more resolved. Thus teachers may be as mentally or emotionally troubled themselves, or 'stuck' where they were, as children.

So teachers do not automatically possess the competences to teach mental, emotional and social health promotion, nor to make the kind of personal adjustments needed to respond to these new demands. For many teachers, working in this area may be a life-changing experience involving the whole self. It can make us reflect on who we fundamentally are; it involves struggle and personal change, and is thus potentially threatening and disturbing (Sylwester 1995). Teachers will not be able to make the necessary changes without active help.

Teacher education and professional development have always been seen as having a central role to play in the health promoting school concept, helping teachers to build their own capacities, equip themselves, gather new ideas, feel more confident and competent, and adjust to change (Chalk and Smith 1995). The ENHPS has placed great emphasis on the role of education, and has set up some major international educational initiatives on school health education in general (Metcalfe et al. 1993), and on mental and emotional health education in particular (Weare and Gray 1994). This education has been seen as a priority in most of the participating countries (WHO 1997b) and shown to be beneficial in bringing together personnel from different countries, and in ensuring continuity, mutual learning and the dissemination of best practice across Europe (Parsons et al. 1997).

The benefits of teacher education

Specific work to develop the emotional and social competences of teachers has proved to be a highly effective way of improving these competences in pupils. Taylor and Hoedt (1974) compared the effectiveness of group counselling of the parents and teachers of children with classroom behaviour problems with group counselling with the children themselves, and showed that counselling the adults was the more effective. In a now classic study, Aspey and Roebuck (1977) demonstrated that staff benefit personally and professionally from developing relationship skills themselves. This study looked at the quality of teaching in a number of schools and showed how essential it is that teachers have good relationship skills, and that, in particular, teachers are able to express empathy, genuineness and respect. Their research showed that, without special training, most of the teachers in their study were not skilled at relating to others, and acted in a way that tended to hold most pupils back rather than help them learn. (It must be said that the teachers were typical of the general population in this respect.) The good news was that the teachers could be educated to improve their skills, and that when they were, the effects on the pupils' learning and behaviour were dramatic: pupils' attendance, effort, achievement and behaviour improved, and the teachers themselves found their own work more rewarding.

Teachers interested in developing work in this area might do well to seek out courses to support them. Courses have a valuable part to play in providing theory, and practising skills in a safe environment. Appropriate education to support health promotion in general and mental, emotional and social health in particular needs to be built into teacher education in all countries, in initial education, in school workshops, in local in-service provision and in accredited courses in universities and colleges. But it is not enough to send people on courses, there also needs to be on-site coaching in the schools themselves, to give follow-up support and to help teachers to practice the skills. Some of the most successful projects have involved supporting teachers with on-site education and workshops, for example, the Resolving Conflict Creatively Programme from New York (Lantieri and Patti 1996). Otherwise the familiar rift between theory and practice is likely to disillusion teachers on their re-entry (Elias *et al.* 1997).

Appendix
Some agencies concerned with mental, emotional and social health in schools

Health education and promotion

World Health Organisation, CH-1211 Geneva 27, Switzerland. Global remit for health education and health promotion. Overall responsibility for health promoting schools, but mainly devolves this to regions. Its Division of Mental Health includes mental health in schools in its remit and mainly uses a life skills approach. It produces a newsletter about school education, 'Skills for Life', and produces lists of 'Mental Health Programmes in Schools', using a life skills approach.

World Health Organisation Regional Office for Europe, 8 Scherfigsvey, DK-2100 Copenhagen, Denmark. European remit for health education and health promotion, including in schools and with children and young people. Coordinates the European Network of Health Promoting Schools (ENHPS) as a whole.

Health Education Authority, England, Hamilton House, Mabledon Place, London, WC1H 9TX. Main national body with overall responsibility for school health education in England. Coordinates the English ENHPS and the Healthy Schools Network. Organises annual National Mental Health Day.

Health Education Board for Scotland, Woodburn House, Canaan Lane, Edinburgh, EH10 4SG. Main national body with overall responsibility for school health education in Scotland. Coordinates the Scottish ENHPS.

Health Promotion Agency for Northern Ireland, 18 Ormeau Avenue, Belfast, BT2 8HS. Main national body with overall responsibility for school health education in Northern Ireland. Coordinates the Northern Ireland ENHPS.

Health Promotion Wales, Ffynnon-las, Ty Glas Avenue, Llanishen, Cardiff, CF4 5DZ. Main national body with overall responsibility for school health education in Wales. Coordinates the Welsh ENHPS.

Mental health

Mind (The National Association for Mental Health), 15–19 Broadway, London, E15 4BQ. Remit for mental health in general for England and Wales. Organises conferences and courses, provides consultancy and advice, publishes books and leaflets, and resources lists of books and resources from other publishers. Has produced materials for mental health education in secondary schools.

Scottish Association for Mental Health (SAMH), Atlantic House, 38 Gardeners Crescent, Edinburgh, EH3 8DP. Scottish equivalent of Mind.

Northern Ireland Association for Mental Health (NIAMH), 80 University Street, Belfast, BT7 1HE. Northern Ireland equivalent of Mind.

Young Minds Trust, 102–108 Clerkenwell Road, London, SW9 0AL. Branch of Mind which deals specifically with mental health and children and young people. Publishes *Young Minds* magazine. Has remit for whole of the UK.

Mental Health Foundation, 20/21 Cornwall Terrace, London, NW1 4QL. National charity which aims at improving services for those with mental health problems and learning disabilities. Develops community projects, and educates the public, policy-makers and professionals.

Emotional and social health in schools

The Collaborative for the Advancement of Social and Emotional Learning (CASEL), Department of Psychology (M/C285), The University of Illinois in Chicago, 1007 W. Harrison Street, Chicago, IL 60607–78137. Major US network of educators, academics and professionals who are engaged in promoting social and emotional learning in schools. Web-site has details of a vast number of projects worldwide, offprints of articles and details of ongoing work. Web-site address: http://www.cfapress.org/casel/casel.html

Antidote, The Campaign for Emotional Literacy, The Hub, 3–4 Albion Place, Galena Road, London, W6 0QT. Lobbies for a greater concern with emotional matters, in education and in politics particularly. Organises conferences, talks and seminars, publishes quarterly newsletter and reports.

Self-Esteem Network, 32 Carisbrooke Road, Walthamstow, London, E17 7EF. Aims to promote the importance of self-esteem, including in education. Produces newsletters, workshops, a directory of materials, a list of trainers and courses, and local self-esteem circles. Now merged with Antidote.

Re:Membering Education, 66 Beaconsfield Villas, Brighton, BN1 6HE. Promotes a concern with relationships in education.

Forum for the Advancement of Educational Therapy and Therapeutic Training, 15 Church Row, London, NW3 6UP and 3 Templewood, Ealing, London, W13 8BA. Aims include promoting insight of teachers into emotional factors in learning and failure to learn. Provides training and in-service education.

Human Scale Education, 96 Carlingott, nr Bath, BA2 8AW. Promotes a concern with a holistic, person-centred approach to education, which emphasises the importance of relationships and the environment. Produces a newsletter, and organises conferences and meetings, including local groups.

Third Ear, PO Box 24000, London, NW4 3WX and 44 Stanley Road, Whitstable, Kent. Promotes the importance of listening (as opposed to talking) in schools, and in psycho-therapy generally. Produces publications.

Social Competences Centre, 75 Willowbrae Avenue, Edinburgh, EH8 7HX and Psychology Dept, University of Dundee, Dundee, Scotland, DD1 4HN. Scottish project on uncovering and disseminating work on social and emotional competences in schools. Has a major web-site with a large searchable database of projects, papers, materials and newsletters. Website address: http://dundee.ac.uk/psychology/prosoc.html

Learning Through Action Trust, Fair Cross, Stratfield Saye, Reading, RG7 2BT. Offers interactive in-service education and consultancy, in the community, and in schools on social and emotional education.

Family Links, The Office, The Old Rectory, Waterstock, Oxfordshire, OX33 1JT. Runs courses for teachers, health professionals and families on nurturing and relationship skills, using a whole school approach, with the aim of creating a calm and disciplined school community.

Counselling

Youth Access, Magazine Business Centre, 11 Newark St, Leicester, LE1 5SS. National network of informal youth counselling, information and advice.

Relate, National Marriage Guidance, Herbert Gray College, Little Church Street, Rugby, Warwickshire, CV21 3AP. Basic work on counselling adult couples, which is supported by concern with relationships education in schools. Runs workshops for teachers and produces lists of resources and books in the field.

British Association of Counselling, 1 Regent Place, Rugby, Warwickshire, CV21 2PJ. Main national body promoting counselling in the UK, including in schools.

Care and welfare of children

National Society for the Prevention of Cruelty to Children, 83 North Street, Bedminster, Bristol, BS3 1ES. General work on child welfare includes projects and training on counselling in schools.

Childline, Royal Mail Building, Studd Street, London, N1 0QW. Work on child protection and the prevention of child abuse, with a focus on the needs and involvement of children. Produces materials for children, and 'accessible' studies, including seeking and publicising the views of children themselves. Working on school-based projects in partnership with schools.

Specific mental and emotional health problems

CRUSE, Cruse House, 126 Sheen Road, Richmond, Surrey, TW9 1UR. General work on bereavement counselling, including a concern to help bereaved children. Trains counsellors to work with bereaved children and young people. Produces a list of published resources on this issue.

The Samaritans, 10 The Grove, Slough, SL1 1QP. Major national telephone service for those who are depressed or suicidal, which is supported by drop-in centres, publications, fact sheets and resources lists, including on suicide and young people.

Depression Alliance, 35 Westminster Bridge Road, London, SE1 7JB. A self-help organisation for people suffering from depression, and for their carers. Publishes a reading and resource list, a quarterly newsletter and leaflets, including on depression and young people. Operates young members pen-friend service.

No Panic, 93 Brands Farm Way, Telford, Shropshire, England, TF3 2JQ. Aims to help people, including young people, suffering from panic attacks, phobias, obsessive–compulsive disorders and tranquilliser use. Provides telephone helpline, drop in-centres and information.

Eating Disorders Association, First Floor, Wensum House, 103 Prince of Wales Road, Norwich, NR1 1DW. Provides help and promotes understanding of anorexia and bulimia, including in children and young people, focusing on their underlying emotional causes. Provides a national network of self-help groups, telephone helplines, information on eating disorders, newsletters, training courses and a professional journal.

Good Grief Publishers, Uxbridge, Middlesex. Publish curriculum materials on helping children and young people cope with grief.

Cooperation, citizenship, conflict resolution and mediation

Brahma Kumaris World Spiritual University, 65 Pound Lane, London, NW10 and 20 Polwarth Crescent, Edinburgh. International organisation on the roster of the United Nations Economic and Social Council, dedicated to the promotion of peace, cooperation and social and spiritual values. Organises conferences, courses and projects, including those with a focus on schools.

The Centre for Citizenship Studies in Education, School of Education, 21 University Road, Leicester, LE1 7RF. Promotes citizenship education in schools through research, projects and publications.

The Values Education Council, c/o Faculty of Education, University of Central England, Westbourne Road, Edgbaston, Birmingham, B15 3TN. Promotes values of social responsibility, caring, participation and pluralism in society through education. Provides a network for the exchange of information and discussion.

National Coalition Building Institute, PO Box 411, Leicester, LE4 8ZY. Dedicated to ending the mistreatment of all groups. Provides training in the skills of prejudice reduction, group conflict resolution and community and coalition building, including in schools.

Mediation UK, Alexander House, Telephone Avenue, Bristol, BS1 4BS. An umbrella organisation and network of projects, organisations and individuals interested in mediation and conflict resolution, including those based in schools.

Community Education and Development Centre, Woodway Park School and Community College, Wigston Road, Coventry. Promotes links between schools, families and the community, and promotes wider access to learning. Organises projects, provides training and consultancy, and publishes books.

Preventing disruption, violence and bullying

Forum on Children and Violence, 8 Wakley Street, London, EC1V 7QE. Network of people committed to the creation of a non-violent society through education. Publishes twice yearly newsletter

Fronting the Challenge, 44 Southdown Road, London, SW20 8PT. Offers training on coping with disruptive pupils by 'developing positive responses to behaviours that interrupt learning'.

Kidscape, 152 Buckingham Palace Road, London, SW1W 9TR. Concerned to prevent bullying in schools. Provides information, training packs and courses.

Sexuality

Family Planning Association, 2–12 Pentonville Road, London, N1 9FP. General work on sexuality and contraception includes a concern with young people. Provides advice, consultancy, training courses and publications.

Brook Advisory Centres, 165 Gray's Inn Road, London, WC1X 8UD. Promotes the education of young people on responsible sexuality and contraception. Network of advisory centres, and produces resources and publications.

Research in mental, emotional and social health in schools

Schools Health Education Unit, University of Exeter, St Luke's, Heavitree Road, Exeter, Devon, EX1 2LU. Ongoing collection and publication of data from an annual survey on the health behaviours and beliefs of young people, including in relation to self-esteem, anxiety and bullying.

Health Education Unit, Research and Graduate School of Education, University of Southampton, Highfield, Southampton, SO17 1BJ. Research into the beliefs, understandings and behaviours of children, young people and their teachers in relation to mental, emotional and social health, and work on developing and evaluating whole school programmes and teacher education on this issue. Produced 'Health for Life', a comprehensive primary school project, and 'Promoting Mental and Emotional Health in the ENHPS', a European teacher education project, with the WHO.

Health Services Research Unit, Department of Public Health, University of Oxford, Institute of Health Sciences, Old Road, Headington, Oxford, OX3 7LF. Undertakes systematic reviews of programmes of emotional and social health in schools, and researches finding ways to measure social and emotional health in individuals.

Further sources of materials

TACADE, 1 Hulme Place, the Crescent, Salford, Greater Manchester, M5 5QA. Consultants to the WHO Division of Mental Health and Substance Abuse in Geneva. Developed their life skills approach to this issue in schools. Produced two teaching packs, 'Skills for the Primary School Child' and 'Skills for Adolescence'.

Lifeskills Associates, Wharfebank House, Ilkley Road, Otley, Leeds, MS21 3JP. Produce comprehensive packages to teach a wide range of social and affective competences to children, young people and adolescents, using a skills-based approach.

Smallwood Publishing Group, Dover, Kent. Lists books and materials from several publishers on a range of issues, including self-esteem, child abuse, anger control, bereavement, bullying, counselling, handling disruptive children, depression and therapy.

Mental Health Media, 356 Holloway Road, London, N7 6PA. Produce directories of hundreds of videos on a wide range of issues to do with mental heath, including many suitable for use in schools.

References

Adams, J. (1998) *Girl Power: How Far Will It Go: A Resource Training Pack on Young Women and Self-Esteem*. Sheffield: Sheffield Centre for HIV and Sexual Health.

Adams, L. and Smithies, J. (1990) *Community Participation and Health Promotion*. London: HEA.

Ainscow, M. (1998) *Towards Effective Schools for All*. London: National Association for SENs.

Ajmal, Y. (1998) ' "Hackney well-being in schools" project'. *Young Minds*, 32, 10–11.

Alberti, R. and Emmons, M. (1974) *Your Perfect Right*. London: Impact Books.

Anderson, B. (1998) 'Mobilising local communities'. *Young Minds*, 34, 16–34.

Anderson, J. (1988) *Health Skills Training Manual*. London: HEA.

Antidote (1998) *Realising the Potential: Emotional Education for All*. London: Antidote.

Antonovsky, A. (1987) *Unravelling the Mystery of Health: How People Manage Stress and Stay Well*. San Francisco: Bass.

Argyle, M. (1985) *The Anatomy of Relationships*. Harmondsworth: Penguin.

Argyle, M., Martin, M. and Lu, L. (1995) 'Testing for stress and happiness: the role of social and cognitive factors'. C. Spielberger and I. Sarason (eds) *Stress and Emotion*, 15, 173–87, Washington DC: Taylor & Francis.

Arora, C. (1994) 'Is there any point in trying to reduce bullying in secondary schools? A two year follow-up of a whole-school anti-bullying policy in one school'. *Educational Psychology in Practice*, 10, 155–62.

Aspey, D. and Roebuck, F. (1977) *Kids Don't Learn From People They Don't Like*. Massachusetts: Human Resource Development Press.

Ausubel, D.P., Novak, J.S. and Hanesian, H. (1978) *Educational Psychology, A Cognitive View*. 2nd edn. New York: Holt, Rinehart & Winston.

Bachmann R. (1986) 'Ecology in the school environment'. *Health Promotion*, 1 (3), 325–34.

Baelz, P.R. (1979) 'The philosophy of health education'. I. Sutherland (ed.) *Health Education Perspectives and Choices*. London: Allen & Unwin.

Balding, J. (1998) *Young People in 1997*. Exeter: University of Exeter, Health Education Unit.

Ball, J. (1998) *School Inclusion: The School, the Family and the Community*. London: Joseph Rowntree Foundation.

Bandura, A. (1977) 'Self-efficacy: toward a unifying theory of behavioural change'. *Psychological Review*, 64 (2), 191–215.

Barr, C. (1985) 'The relationship of physical activity and exercise to mental health'. *Public Health Report*, 100 (2), 195–202.

Battistich, V., Watson, M., Solomon, D., Schaps, E. and Solomon, J. (1991) 'The Child Development Project: a comprehensive program for the development of prosocial character'. W. Kurtines and J. Gewirtz (eds) *Handbook of Moral Behavior and Development*. Hillsdale, NJ: Lawrence Erlbaum Associates Inc.

Battistich, V., Solomon, D., Watson, M. and Schaps, E. (1997) 'Caring school communities'. *Educational Psychologist*, 32, (3), 137–51.

Beattie, A. (1991) 'Knowledge and control in health promotion: a test case for social theory and social policy'. J. Gabe, M. Calnan and M. Bury (eds) *Sociology of the Health Service*. London: Routledge.

Becker, M. (1984) *The Health Belief Model and Personal Health Behaviour*. Thorofare, NJ: Charles B. Slack.

Beelmann, A., Pfingsten, U. and Losel, F. (1994) 'Effects of training social competence in children: A meta-analysis of recent evaluation studies'. *Journal of Clinical Child Psychology*, 23, 260–71.

Bender, W. (1987) 'Effective educational practices in the mainstream setting: recommended model for evaluation of mainstream teacher classes'. *The Journal of Special Education*, 20 (4), 475–87.

Benninga, J. and Belli, E. (1982) 'Social development in the classroom'. *Viewpoints in Teaching and Learning*, 58 (1), 128–31.

Benson, A. and Benson, J. (1993) 'Peer mediation: conflict resolution in schools'. *Journal of School Psychology*, 31 (3), 427–30.

Bernstein, B. (1975) *Class, Codes and Control*. London: Routledge.

Besalel-Azrin, V., Azrin, N. and Armstrong, P. (1977) 'The student-oriented classroom: a method of improving student conduct and satisfaction'. *Behavior Therapy*, 8 (2), 193–204.

Blair, M. and Bourne, J. (1998) *Making the Difference: Teaching and Learning Strategies in the Multi-Ethnic School*. Norwich: HMSO.

Borba, M. (1989) *Esteem Builders*. California, USA: Rolling Hills Estates.

Bosma, M.W.M. and Hosman, C.M.H. (1991) *Mental Health Promotion and Prevention in Schools*. Utrecht: Dutch Centre for Health Education and Health Promotion and the WHO Regional Office for Europe.

Botvin, G. and Dusenbury, L. (1989) 'Substance abuse prevention and the promotion of competence'. L. Bond and B. Compas (eds) *Primary Prevention and Promotion in the Schools. Primary Prevention of Psychopathology*, vol. 12. Newbury Park, California: Sage Publications.

Boulton, M. and Flemington, I. (1996) 'The effects of a short video intervention on secondary-school pupils' involvement in, definitions of, and attitudes towards, bullying'. *School Psychology International*, 17 (4), 331–45.

Bowers, L., Smith, P. and Binney, V. (1994) 'Perceived family relationships of bullies, victims and bully/victims in middle childhood'. *Journal of Social and Personal Relationships*, 11 215–32.

Bowlby, J. (1980) *Attachment and Loss*. London: Hogarth.

Brahma Kumaris (1995) *Living Values: A Guidebook*. London: Brahma Kumaris World Spiritual University.

Bremner, W. (1999) *Promoting Social Competence*. Dundee: University of Dundee.

Brendtro, L., Brokenleg, M. and Van Bockern, S. (1990) *Reclaiming Youth at Risk: Our Hope for the Future*. Bloomington, IN: National Education Service.

Bretherton, D., Collins, L. and Ferretti, C. (1993) 'Dealing with conflict: assessment of a course for secondary school students'. *Australian Psychologist*, 28 (2), 105–111.

Briggs, S., MacKay, T. and Miller, S. (1995) 'The Edinbarnet Playground Project: changing aggressive behaviour through structured intervention'. *Educational Psychology in Practice*, 11, 37–44.

Brigham,T. (1989) *Self-management for Adolescents: A Skills-training Program*. New York: Guilford Press.

Bruner, J. (1966) *Towards a Theory of Instruction*. Cambridge: Harvard University Press.

Brunn Jensen, B. (1997) 'A case of two paradigms within health education'. *Health Education Research*, 12 (4), 419–28.

Bruun Jensen, B. (1994) 'An action competence approach to health education'. C. Chu and R. Simpson (eds) *Ecological Public Health: From Vision to Practice*. Brisbane: Griffiths University.

Bryk, A. and Driscoll, M. (1988) *The High School as Community: Contextual Influences and Consequences for Students and Teachers*. Madison: National Center on Effective Secondary Schools.

Buck, B. and Inman, S. (1992) *Whole School Provision for Personal and Social Education: The Role of Cross Curricular Elements*. London: Goldsmiths College.

Buckroyd, J. (1996) *Anorexia and Bulimia*. London: Element.

Buell, G. and Snyder, J. (1981) 'Assertiveness training with children'. *Psychological Reports*, 49 (1), 71–80.

Bunton, R. and Macdonald, D. (eds) (1992) *Health Promotion: Disciplines and Diversity*. London: Routledge.

Burley-Allen, M. (1982) *Listening: the Forgotten Skill*. New York: John Wiley.

Burningham, S. (1994) *Young People Under Stress*. London: Virago.

Butler, G. and Hope, T. (1995) *Manage Your Mind: The Mental Fitness Guide*. Oxford: Oxford University Press.

Caplan, M., Weissberg, R., Grober, J., Sivo, P., Grady, K. and Jacoby, C. (1992) 'Social competence promotion with inner-city and suburban young adolescents – effects on social-adjustment and alcohol-use'. *Journal of Consulting and Clinical Psychology*, 60 (1), 56–63.

Caplan, R. and Holland, R. (1990) 'Rethinking health education theory'. *Health Education Journal*, 49, 10–12.

Carey, S. and Stoner, G. (1994) 'Contextual considerations in social skills instruction'. *School Psychology Quarterly*, 9 (2), 137–41.

Carkuff, R. (1985) *The Art of Helping*. Amerhurst: Human Resource Development Press.

CASEL (1998) *The Collaborative for the Advancement of Social and Emotional Learning*. Chicago: University of Illinois in Chicago. Web-site address: http://www.cfapress.org/casel/casel.html

Catford, J. and Parish, R. (1989) ' "Heartbeat Wales", new horizons for health promotion in the community – the philosophy and practice of Heartbeat Wales'. D. Seedhouse and A. Cribb (eds) *Changing Ideas In Health Care*. Chichester: John Wiley.

Chalk, M. and Smith, H. (1995) 'Training professionals to run social skills groups for children'. *Educational Psychology in Practice*, 11 (2), 30–36.

Chapman, S., Lister-Sharpe, D., Sowden, A. and Stewart-Brown, S. (1999) *Systematic Review of Reviews of Health Promotion in Schools*. York: Centre for Reviews and Dissemination, University of York.

Church, A., Edwards, L. and Romain, E. (1990) *Cooperation in the Classroom*. London, Brahma Kumaris World Spiritual University: Global Cooperation for a Better World.

Chwedorowicz, A. (1992) 'Psychic hygiene in mental health promotion'. D. Trent (ed.) *Promotion of Mental Health*, vol. 1. Aldershot: Avebury.

Clarity Collective (1988) *Taught Not Caught: Strategies for Sex Education*. 2nd edn. Cambridge: LDA.

Clayton, R., Cattarello, A. and Johnstone, B. (1996) 'The effectiveness of drug-abuse resistance education (project DARE) – 5-year follow-up results'. *Preventive Medicine*, 25 (3), 307–18.

Cleary, H., Kitchen, J. and Ensor, P. (eds) (1985) *Advancing Health Through Education: A Case Study Approach*. Palo Alto: Mayfield.

Coard, B. (1971) *How the West Indian Child is Made Educationally Subnormal in the British School System*. London: Writers and Readers Cooperative.

Cochran, L., Feng, H., Cartledge, G. and Hamilton, S. (1993) 'The effects of cross-age tutoring on the academic achievement, social behaviors, and self-perceptions of low-achieving African–American males with behavioral disorders'. *Behavioral Disorders*, 18, 292–302.

Coggans, N. and McKellar S. (1995) *Health Promoting Schools*. Strathclyde: Department of Pharmaceutical Sciences, University of Strathclyde.

Cohen, J. (1993) *Handbook of School-Based Interventions: Resolving Student Problems and Promoting Healthy Educational Environments*. San Francisco: Jossey-Bass.

Cohen, S. (1995) (ed.) *WHO Expert Committee on Comprehensive School Health Education and Promotion. Background Working Document 3*. Newton, MA: Health and Human Development Programmes.

Coleman, J. (1997) *Key Data on Adolesence*. Brighton: Trust for the Study of Adolescence.

Coleman, J. and Hendry, L. (1990) *The Nature of Adolescence*. 2nd edn. London: Routledge.

Coleman, M., Wheeler, L. and Webber, J. (1993) 'Research on interpersonal problem-solving training: a review'. *RASE Remedial and Special Education*, 14 (2), 15–30.

Commission of the European Communities (1990) *Healthy Schools, Proceedings of the First European Conference on Health Promotion and the Prevention of Cancer in Schools, Dublin, 1990*. Brussels: Commission of the European Communities.

Coopersmith, S. (1967) *The Antecedents of Self-Esteem*. New York: W.H. Freeman and Co.

Cribb, A. and Dines, A. (1993) 'What is health?'. A. Dines and A. Cribb (eds) *Health Promotion Concepts and Practice*. London: Blackwell Scientific Publications.

Csikszentmihalyi, M. (1990) *Flow: The Psychology of Optimal Experience*. New York: Harper & Row.

Cullingford, J. (1985) (ed.) *Parents, Teachers and Schools*. London: Royce.

Cytryn, L. (1997) *Growing Up Sad: Childhood Depression and its Treatment.* London: Norton.

Damasio, A. (1994) *Descartes' Error: Emotion, Reason and the Human Brain.* New York: Grosset/Putnam.

Davis, J. and Macdonald, G. (1998) *Quality, Evidence and Effectiveness in Health Promotion.* London: Routledge.

Davison, C., Frankel, S. and Davey Smith, G. (1992) 'The limits of lifestyle: reassessing "fatalism" in the popular culture of illness prevention'. *Social Science and Medicine*, 34 (6), 675–85.

Daw, R. and Joyce, R. (1996) 'Drug awareness for parents'. *Health Education*, May, pp. 8–11.

Dean, C. (1995) 'Angry adieu to years of experience'. *Times Educational Supplement*, 4120, 16 January, pp. 4–5.

Dean, K. and Hancock, T. (1992) *Supportive Environments for Health.* Copenhagen: WHO Regional Office for Europe.

Department of Education and Science (1989) *English for Ages 5 to 16.* London: HMSO.

Devlin, T. (1998) *Public Relations and Marketing for Schools.* London: Pitman.

Dickinson, A. (1982) *A Woman in Your Own Right.* London: Quartet.

Diener, E. and Larsen, R. (1993) 'The experience of emotional well-being'. M. Lewis and J. Havilland (eds) *Handbook of Emotions.* New York: Guildford Press.

DoH (Department of Health) (1992) *The Health of the Nation.* London: HMSO.

Donaldson, R.J. and Donaldson, L.J. (1993) *Essential Public Health Medicine.* London: Kluwer Academic Publishers.

Dong, Y., Hallberg, E., Hassard, J. and Harvey, J. (1979) 'Effects of assertion training on aggressive behavior of adolescents'. *Journal of Counseling Psychology*, 2 (5), 459–61.

Douglas (1964) *The Home and the School.* London: MacGibbon and Kee.

Downie, R.S., Fyfe, C. and Tannahill, A. (1990) *Health Promotion Models and Values.* Oxford: Oxford University Press.

Dryden, W. (1995) *Rational Emotive Behaviour Therapy.* London: Sage Publications.

Duck, S. (1983) *Friends, for Life: The Psychology of Close Relationships.* Brighton: Harvester.

Dukes, R., Ullman, J. and Stein, J. (1996) '3-year follow-up of drug abuse resistance education (DARE)'. *Evaluation Review*, 20 (1), 49–66.

DuPaul, G. and Eckert, T. (1994) 'The effects of social skills curricula: now you see them, now you don't'. *School Psychology Quarterly*, 9 (2), 113–32.

Durlak, C., Rose, E. and Bursuck, W. (1994) 'Preparing high school students with learning disabilities for the transition to post-secondary education: teaching the skills of self-determination'. *Journal of Learning Disabilities*, 27 (1), 51–9.

Durlak, J. (1995) *School Based Prevention Programmes for Children and Adolescents.* London: Sage.

Durlak, J. and Wells, A. (1997) 'Primary prevention mental health programs for children and adolescents: a meta-analytic review'. *American Journal of Community Psychology*, 25 (2), 115–52.

Dwivedi, K. (1988) *Group Work with Children and Adolescents.* London: Jessica Kingsley.

Dyregrov, A. (1990) *Grief in Children*. London: Jessica Kingley.

Egan, G. (1998) *The Skilled Helper: A Problem Managment Approach to Helping*. 6th edn. Pacific Grove, California: Brooks/Cole.

Eitan, T., Amir, Y. and Rich, Y. (1992) 'Social and academic treatments in mixed ethnic classes and change in student self-concept'. *British Journal of Educational Psychology*, 62 (3), 364–74.

Ekman, P., Friesen, W. and Ellsworth, P. (1972) *Emotions in the Human Face*. New York: Pergamon.

Elias, M. (1997) 'The missing piece: making the case for greater attention to social and emotional learning'. *Casel Collections*, vol. 1, edn 1.2. Chicago, IL: The Collaborative for the Advancement of Social and Emotional Learning (CASEL).

Elias, M. (1995) 'Primary prevention as health and social competence promotion'. *Journal of Primary Prevention*, 16, 5–24.

Elias, M. (1990) 'The role of affect and social relationships in health behaviour and school health curriculum and instruction'. *Journal of School Health*, 60 (4), 157–63.

Elias, M. and Allen, G. (1991) 'A comparison of instructional methods for delivering a preventive social competence/social decision-making program to at-risk, average, and competent students'. *School Psychology Quarterly*, 6 (4), 251–72.

Elias, M., Gara, M., Schuyler, T., Branden-Muller, L. and Sayette, M. (1991) 'The promotion of social competence: longitudinal study of a preventive school-based program'. *American Journal of Orthopsychiatry*, 61 (3), 409–17.

Elias, M. and Kress, J. (1994) 'Social decision-making and life skills development: a critical thinking approach to health promotion in the middle school'. *Journal of School Health*, 64 (2), 62–66.

Elias, M. and Tobias, S. (1996) *Social Problem Solving: Interventions in Schools*. New York: Guildford.

Elias, M., Weissberg, R., Zins, J., Kendall, P., Dodge, K., Jason, L., Rotheramborus, M., Perry, C., Hawkins, J. and Gottfredson, D. (1996) 'Transdisciplinary collaboration among school researchers – the consortium on the school-based promotion of social competence'. *Journal of Educational and Psychological Consultation*, 7 (1), 25–39.

Elias, M., Zins, J., Weissberg, R., Frey, K., Greenberg, M., Haynes, N., Kessler, R., Schwab-Stone, M. and Shriver, T. (1997) *Promoting Social and Emotional Learning*. Alexandria, Virginia: ASCD.

Elton, Lord (1989) *Discipline in Schools: Report of the Committee of Enquiry Chaired by Lord Elton*. London: HMSO.

Enger, J. (1995) *Violence Prevention in the Middle Level Curriculum: Student Characteristics and Acquisition of Knowledge about Violence*. Paper presented at the Annual Meeting of the American Educational Research Association, San Francisco, CA, 18–22 April 1995.

Epstein, T. and Elias, M. (1996) 'To reach for the stars. How social/affective education can foster truly inclusive environments'. *PHI Delta Kappan*, 78 (2), 157–62.

Erikson, E. (1977) *Childhood and Society*. London: Palladin.

Erikson, E. (1968) *Identity, Youth and Crisis*. London: Faber & Faber.

Family Links (1999) *Information Leaflet on Family Link: the Nuturing Programme for Schools*. Oxford: Family Links.

Fantuzzo, J., Polite, K. C., David, M. and Quinn, G. (1988) 'An evaluation of the effectiveness of teacher- vs. student-management classroom interventions'. *Psychology in the Schools*, 25, 154–63.

Farivar, S. (1991) *Intergroup Relations in Cooperative Learning Groups*. Paper presented at the Annual Meeting of the American Educational Research Association, Chicago, IL, 3–7 April 1991.

Farley, P. (1987) 'English and health education'. K. David and T. Williams (eds) *Health Education in Schools*. Cambridge: Harper & Row.

Felsman, J.K. and Valliant, G.E. (1987) 'Resilient children as adults: a 40 year study'. E. Anderson and B. Cohler (eds) *The Invulnerable Child*. New York: Guildford.

Ferrentino, M. (1990) *Increasing Social Competence in Kindergarten and First Grade Children through Modeling and Practice in a Self-Motivating Play Group*. Ed.D. Thesis, Nova University.

Fertman, C. and Chubb, N. (1992) 'The effects of a psycho-educational program on adolescents' activity involvement, self-esteem and locus of control'. *Adolescence*, 27 (107), 517–26.

Fletcher-Campbell, F. with Hall, C. (1993) *LEA Support for Special Needs*. London: NFER/Nelson.

Fodor, I. (ed.) (1992) *Adolescent Assertiveness and Social Skills Training: A Clinical Handbook*. New York: Springer.

Foltz-Gray, D. (1996) 'The bully trap: young tormentors and their victims find ways out of anger and isolation'. *Teaching Tolerance*, 5, 18–23.

Foster, P., Gomm, R. and Hammersley, M. (1996)*Constructing Educational Inequality*. London: Falmer Press.

Franca, V., Kerr, M., Reitz, A. and Lambert, D. (1990) 'Peer tutoring among behaviorally disordered students: academic and social benefits to tutor and tutee'. *Education and Treatment of Children*, 13, 109–28.

Fraser, B. and Walberg, H. (eds) (1991) *Educational Environments*. Oxford: Pergamon.

Frederickson, N. and Simms, J. (1990) 'Teaching social skills to children: towards an integrated approach'. *Educational and Child Psychology*, 7 (1), 5–17.

Freire, P. (1973) *Education and the Practice of Freedom*. London: Writers and Readers Publishing Cooperative.

Freud, S. (1957) 'The unconcious'. J. Strachey (ed. and translator) *The Standard Edition of the Complete Works of Sigmund Freud*. London: Hogarth.

Fuchs, E. (1973) 'How teachers learn to help pupils fail'. N. Keddie (ed.) *Tinker-Tailor … the Myth of Cultural Deprivation*. Harmondsworth: Penguin.

Furlong, M. and Smith, D. (eds) (1994) *Anger, Hostility, and Aggression: Assessment, Prevention, and Intervention Srategies for Youth*. Brandon, VT: Clinical Psychology. Publishing Company.

Gable, R., Arllen, N. and Hendrickson, J. (1994) 'Use of students with emotional/behavioral disorders as behavior change agents'. *Education and Treatment of Children*, 17, 267–76.

Gagne, R. (1965) *The Conditions of Learning*. New York: Holt, Rinehart & Winston.

Gardner, H. (1993a) *Frames of Mind: The Theory of Multiple Intelligences*. 2nd edn. Glasgow: Fontana.

Gardner, H. (1993b) *The Multiple Intelligences: The Theory in Practice*. New York: Basic Books.

Gardner, H., Kornhaber, M. and Wake, W. (1995) *Intelligence: Multiple Perspectives*. London: Harcourt Brace College Publishers.

Geldard, K. and Geldard, D. (1997) *Counselling Children*. London: Sage Publications.

Gentry, D. and Benenson, W. (1992) 'School-age peer mediators transfer knowledge and skills to home setting'. *Mediation Quarterly*, 10, 101–9.

Gettinger, M., Doll, B. and Salmon, D. (1994) 'Effects of social problem solving, goal setting, and parent training on children's peer relations'. *Journal of Applied Developmental Psychology*, 15 (2), 141–63.

Gillborn, D. (1990) *'Race', Ethnicity and Education*. London: Unwin Hyman.

Giuliano, J. (1994) 'A peer education-program to promote the use of conflict-resolution skills among at-risk school-age males'. *Public Health Reports*, 109 (2), 158–61.

Glaser, R. and Kiecolt-Glaser, J. (1987) 'Stress associated depression in cellular immunity'. *Brain, Behaviour and Immunity*, 1, 107–112.

Goleman, D. (1996) *Emotional Intelligence*. London: Bloomsbury.

Goodman, G., Powell, E. and Burke, J. (1989) 'The buddy system: a reintegration technique'. *Academic Therapy*, 25, 195–9.

Gordon, J. and Grant, G. (1997) *How We Feel*. London: Jessica Kingsley.

Gottfredson, D., Gottfredson, G. and Hybl, L. (1993) 'Managing adolescent behavior: a multiyear, multischool study'. *American Educational Research Journal*, 30, 179–215.

Graham, H. (1984) *Women, Health and the Family*. Brighton: Wheatsheaf Books.

Graham, P. and Rutter, M. (1970) 'Identification of children with psychiatric disorder'. M. Rutter, J. Tizard and K. Whitemore (eds) *Education, Health and Behaviour*. London: Longman.

Gray, J. (1994) *Men are from Mars, Women are from Venus*. New York: Thorsons.

Greenberg, M. and Kusche, C. (1993) *Promoting Social and Emotional Development in Deaf Children: the PATHS project*. Seattle: University of Washington Press.

Greenberg, M., Kusche, C., Cook, E. and Quamma, J. (1995) 'Promoting emotional competence in school-aged children – the effects of the paths curriculum'. *Development and Psychopathology*, 7 (1), 117–36.

Greenberg, M. and Snell, J. (1997) 'Brain development and emotional development: the role of teaching in organising the frontal lobe'. P. Salovey and S. Sluyter (eds) *Emotional Development and Emotional Intelligence: Implications for Educators*. New York: Basic Books.

Greene, B. and Uroff, S. (1991) 'Quality education and at risk students'. *Journal of Reality Therapy*, 10, 3–11.

Greenhalgh, P. (1994) *Emotional Growth and Learning*. London: Routledge.

Grossman, P. and Hughes, J. (1992) 'Self-control interventions with internalizing disorders – a review and analysis'. *School Psychology Review*, 21 (2), 229–45.

Growald, E. (1998) 'A case for emotional literacy'. *Casel Collections*, vol. 1, edn 1.4. Chicago, IL: The Collaborative for the Advancement of Social and Emotional Learning (CASEL).

Gurney, P. (1988) *Self-Esteem in Children with Special Educational Needs.* London: Routledge.

Guttman, C. (1994) *On the Right Track: Servol's Early Childhood and Adolescent Development Programmes in Trinidad and Tobago. Education for All: Making It Work. Innovations Series, 5.* Paris: UNESCO, Basic Education Division.

Haertel, G., Walberg, H. and Haertel, E. (1981) 'Socio-psychological environments and learning: a quantitative analysis'. *British Educational Research Journal,* 7, 27–36.

Hagquist, C. and Starrin, B. (1997) 'Health education in schools: from information to empowerment models'. *Health Promotion International,* 12 (3), 225–32.

Hains, A. (1992) 'Comparison of cognitive–behavioral stress management techniques with adolescent boys'. *Journal of Counseling and Development,* 70 (5), 600–605.

Hall, E., Hall, C. and Ramazn, A. (1997) 'The effects of human relations training on reported teacher stress, pupil control ideology and locus of control'. *Research in Education,* 57, 57–66.

Hamacheck, D. (1978) *Encounters with the Self.* New York: Holt, Rhinehart & Winston.

Hammond, W. and Yung, B. (1991) 'Preventing violence in at-risk African–American youth. Conference: pursuing the health and development of young African–American males'. *Journal of Health Care for the Poor and Underserved,* 2, 359–73.

Hargreaves, D. (1967) *Social Relations in the Secondary School.* London: Routledge.

Harris C. (1991) *A Green School.* Sheffield: Scholastic Publications.

Hartley-Brewer, E. (1997) 'Motivation: a five stage model'. *Young Minds,* 33, 14–16.

Harvard and WHO (1996) *Global Burden of Disease.* Geneva: WHO.

Haviland-Jones, J., Gebalt, J. and Stapley, J. (1997) 'The questions of development in emotion'. P. Salovey and S. Sluyter (eds) *Emotional Development and Emotional Intelligence: Implications for Educators.* New York: Basic Books.

Hawkins, J. and Catalano, R. (1992) *Communities That Care: Action for Drug Abuse Prevention.* San Francisco: Jossey-Bass.

Hayden, C. (1997) *Children Excluded from Primary School.* Milton Keynes: Open University.

Hayes, E., Cunningham, G. and Robinson, J. (1977) 'Counseling focus: are parents necessary?'. *Elementary School Guidance and Counseling,* 12, 8–14.

Haynes, N. and Comer, J. (1996) 'Integrating schools, families and communities through successful school reform'. *School Psychology Review,* 25, 4.

HEA (1999) *Whole School, Healthy School: An Essential Guide to the Health Promoting School.* London: HEA.

HEA (1999) *Young People and Health: Health Behaviour in School-Aged Children.* London: HEA.

HEA (1997) *Mental Health Promotion: A Quality Framework.* London: HEA.

HEA (1995a) *The European Network of Health Promoting Schools: Development Planning Review Days: Feedback Report and Research Report.* London: HEA.

HEA (1995b) *The European Network of Health Promoting Schools: Manchester Network Event: Feedback Report.* London: HEA.

HEA (1989) *Health For Life: The HEA Primary School Project.* Walton-on-Thames: Thomas Nelson.

HEA and NFER (1997a) *The Health Promoting School: Final Report of the ENHPS Evaluation in England*. London: HEA.

HEA and NFER (1997b) *Parents' Views of Health Education*. London: HEA.

Henderson, P., Kelbey, T. and Engebretson, K. (1992) 'Effects of a stress-contol program on children's locus of control, self-concept, and coping behavior'. *School Counselor*, 40 (2), 125–30.

Hendren, R., Birell Weisen, R. and Orley, J. (1994) *Mental Health Programmes in Schools*. Geneva: WHO, Division of Mental Health and Substance Abuse.

Herman, J. (1994) *Trauma and Recovery*. London: Pandora.

Hoffman, M. (1984) 'Empathy, social cognition and moral action'. W. Kurtines and J. Gerwitz (eds) *Moral Behaviour and Moral Development: Advances in Theory, Research and Applications*. New York: John Wiley.

Holden, R. (1998) *Happiness Now*. London: Hodder and Stoughton.

Hollin, C. (1990) 'Social skills training with delinquents: A look at the evidence and some recommendations for practice'. *British Journal of Social Work*, 20, 483–93.

Hon, C. and Watkins, D. (1995) 'Evaluating a social skills training program for Hong Kong students'. *Journal of Social Psychology*, 135, 527–28.

Hopson, B. and Scally, M. (1981) *Lifeskills Teaching*. London: McGraw Hill.

Hord, S., Rutherford, W., Huling-Austin, L. and Hall, G. (1987) *Taking Charge of Change*. Alexandria: ASCD.

Hosman, C. and Veltman, N. (1994) *Prevention in Mental Health: A Review of the Effectiveness of Health Education and Health Promotion*. Utrecht: Dutch Centre for Health Promotion and Health Education.

Houghton, S. (1991) 'Promoting generalization of appropriate behaviour across special and mainstream settings: a case study'. *Educational Psychology in Practice*, 7 (1), 49–53.

Hoy, W., Tarter, J. and Kottkamp, B. (1991) *Open Schools, Healthy Schools: Measuring Organisational Climate*. Newbury Park, CA: Sage Publications.

Huey, W. and Rank, R. (1984) 'Effects of counselor and peer-led group assertive training on Black adolescent aggression'. *Journal of Counseling Psychology*, 31 (1), 95–8.

Hui, E. and Chan, D. (1996) 'Teacher stress and guidance work in Hong Kong secondary school teachers'. *British Journal of Guidance & Counselling*, 24 (2), 199–211.

Hull, T. (1987) 'Science and health education'. K. David and T. Williams (eds) *Health Education in Schools*. Cambridge: Harper and Row.

Hunter, J., Phillips, S. and Wetton, N. (1998) *Hand in Hand: Emotional Development Through Literature*. London: Saffire.

Hymans, M. (1994) 'Impulsive behaviour: A case for helping children "think" about change'. *Educational Psychology in Practice*, 10 (3), 141–8.

Ives, R. and Clements, I. (1996) 'Drug education in schools: a review'. *Children and Society*, 10 (1), 14–27.

James, W. (1890) *Principles of Psychology, 2*. London: Macmillan.

Jelinek, M. (1991) 'The clinician and the randomised control trial'. J. Daly, I. Macdonald and E. Willis (eds) *Researching Health Care: Designs, Dilemmas, Disciplines*. London: Routledge.

Jenkins, K., McCulloch, A. and Parker, C. (1998) *Supporting Governments and Policy Makers: Nations for Mental Health*. Geneva: WHO, Division of Mental Health and Prevention of Substance Abuse.

Johnson, D. and Johnson, R. (1992) *Learning Together and Alone: Cooperative, Competitive and Individualistic Learning*. Needham Heights, MA: Allyn and Bacon.

Johnson, D. and Johnson, R. (1994) 'Cooperative learning and conflict resolution'. *The Fourth R*, 42, 1.

Johnson, D., Johnson, R., Dudley, B. and Burnett, R. (1992) 'Teaching students to be peer mediators'. *Educational Leadership*, 50, 10–13.

Johnson, D., Johnson, R., Dudley, B., Ward, M. and Magnuson, D. (1995) 'The impact of peer mediation training on the management of school and home conflicts'. *American Educational Research Journal*, 32, 829–44.

Johnstone, M. (1992) *Teachers' Workload and Associated Stress*. Edinburgh: Scottish Council for Research in Education.

Jones, C. (1994) *Effects of Values Instruction on Third and Fourth Grade Students*. Paper presented at the Annual Meeting of the Mid-South Research Association, Nashville, TN, 9–11 November 1994.

Jones, R., McDonald, D., Fiore, M. and Arrington, T. (1990) *Journal of Pediatric Psychology*, 15, 211–23.

Journal of School Health (1990) *Comprehensive School Health Programmes: Current Status and Future Prospects*, 60, 4.

Juhan, D. (1987) *Job's Body – A Handbook for Bodywork*. New York: Station Press.

Jupp, J. and Griffiths, M. (1990) 'Self-concept changes in shy, socially isolated adolescents following social skills training emphasising role plays'. *Australian Psychologist*, 25, 165–77.

Kalliopuska, M. and Tiitinen, U. (1991) 'Influence of two developmental programmes on the empathy and prosociability of preschool children'. *Perceptual and Motor Skills*, 72, 323–28.

Kamps, D. and Tankersley, M. (1996) 'Prevention of behavioral and conduct disorders: trends and research issues'. *Behavioral Disorders*, 22 (1), 41–8.

Kane, R. (1994) 'Performing arts: not as mere therapy but as a powerful public force'. D. Trent and C. Reed (eds) *Promotion of Mental Health*, vol. 3. Aldershot: Avebury.

Kavale and Forness (1996) 'Social skill deficits and learning disabilities: a meta-analysis'. *Journal of Learning Disabilities*, 29, 226–37.

Kaye, P. and Webb, A. (1996) ' "A little help from my friends": a secondary school peer support programme'. *Pastoral Care* (June), 21–25.

Keddie, N. (1973) 'Introduction'. N. Keddie (ed.) *Tinker-Tailor … the Myth of Cultural Deprivation*. Harmondsworth: Penguin.

Kellner, M. and Tutin, J. (1995) 'A school-based anger management program for developmentally and emotionally disabled high-school students'. *Adolescence*, 30 (120), 813–25.

Kelly, D. (1997) 'Education and difficult children: the teaching dilemma'. *Young Minds*, 29, 17–18.

Kelly, G. (1955) *The Psychology of Personal Constructs*. New York: Norton.

Kennerley, H. (1997) *Overcoming Anxiety: A Self Help Guide Using Cognitive Behavioural Techniques*. London: Robinson.

Kern, L., Dunlap, G., Childs, K. and Clarke, S. (1994) 'Use of a classwide self-management program to improve the behavior of students with emotional and behavioral disorders'. *Education and Treatment of Children*, 17 (4), 445–58.

Kessler, R. (1997) 'Social and emotional learning. An emerging field builds a foundation for peace'. *Holistic Education*, 10 (4), 4–15.

Ketchel, J. and Bieger, G. (1989) *The efficacy of a psychosocially based drug prevention program for young adolescents*. Paper presented at the Annual Meeting of the New England Educational Research Organization. Portsmouth, NH, 26 April 1989.

Kidscape (1998) *Kidscape Survey on the Long Term Effects of Bullying*. London: Kidscape.

Kim, S., McLeod, J., Rader, D. and Johnston, G. (1992) 'An evaluation of prototype school-based peer counseling program'. *Journal of Drug Education*, 22 (1), 37–53.

Klein, M. (1946) 'Notes on some psychoid mechanisms'. *International Journal of Psycho-Analysis*, 27, 99–110.

Kreidler, W. (1984) *Creative Conflict Resolution: More Than 200 Activities for Keeping Peace in the Classroom*. Glenview, Illinois: Scott Foresman.

Kuhn, T. (1962)*The Structure of Scientific Revolutions*. Chicago: The University Press.

Kyriacou, C. (1996) 'Teacher stress: a review of some international comparisons'. *Education Section Review*, 20 (1) 17–20.

Lane, D. (1989) 'Violent histories: bullying and criminality'. D. Tattum and D. Lane (eds) *Bullying in Schools*. Stoke on Trent: Trentham Books.

Langone, J., Clees, T., Oxford, M. and Malone, M. (1995) 'Acquisition and generalization of social skills by high school students with mild mental retardation'. *Mental Retardation*, 33 186–96.

Lantieri, L. and Patti, J. (1996) *Waging Peace in Our Schools*. Boston: Beacon Press.

Larson, J. (1994) 'Violence prevention in the schools – a review of selected programs and procedures'. *School Psychology Review*, 23 (2), 151–164.

Lawrence, E. (1999) 'Talk it out: conflict management in schools'. *Promoting Social Competence*. Edinburgh: Promoting Social Competences Project.

Lazerson, D. (1980) ' "I must be good if I can teach": peer tutoring with aggressive and withdrawn children'. *Journal of Learning Disabilities*, 13, 152–7.

Lee, J. (1994) 'Prevention, process and product: the role of Life Skills'. In D. Trent and C. Reed (eds) *Promotion of Mental Health*, vol. 3. Aldershot: Avebury.

Leech, A. (1995) 'Missing, presumed ill'. *Education*, 185 (24), 11.

Leenaars, A. and Wenckstern, S. (1991) *Suicide Prevention in Schools*. London: Hemisphere Publishing Corporation.

Leon, G. (1993) 'Personality and behavioural vulnerabilities associated with risk status for eating disorders for adolescent girls'. *Journal of Abnormal Psychology*, 102, 438–44.

Lenton, S. and Midford, R. (1996) 'Clarifying "harm reduction"?' *Drug and Alcohol Review*. 15, 411–13.

Liedekerken, P., Jonkers, R., Haes, W., Kok, G. and Saan, J. (1990) *Effectiveness of Health Education*. Assen, The Netherlands: Van Gorcum.

Lin, R. and Lin, H. (1996) 'A study of junior high school teachers' mental health in Taiwan'. D. Trent and C. Reed (eds) *Promotion of Mental Health*, vol. 5. Aldershot: Avebury.

Little, R. (1982) 'Norms of collegiality and experimentation: workplace conditions of school success'. *American Educational Research*, 78, 178–85.

Loeber, R. (1990) 'Development and risk factors of juvenile antisocial behaviour and delinquency. *Clinical Psychology Review*, 10, 1–41.

Lowenstein, L. (1989) 'The peer group promoting socialised behaviour: How can the peer group be mobilised to counteract and remedy negative behaviour?' *Education Today*, 39 (2), 27–34.

Lowenstein, L. (1983) 'Developing self-control and self-esteem in disturbed children'. *School Psychology International*, 4 (4), 229–36.

Maag, J. (1990) 'Social skills training in schools'. *Special Services in the Schools*, 6 (1–2), 1–19.

Macdonald, G. (1994) 'Self-esteem and the promotion of mental health'. D. Trent and C. Reed (eds) *Promotion of Mental Health*, vol. 3. Aldershot: Avebury.

Macdonald, G. and O'Hara, K. (1998) *Ten Elements of Mental health, its Promotion and Demotion: Implications for Practice*. Glasgow: Society of Health Promotion Specialists.

Maciver, S. (1998) 'Transition groups: a psycho-dynamic approach'. *Young Minds*, 32, 14–15.

Macklem, G. (1987) 'No one wants to play with me'. *Academic Therapy*, 22, 477–84.

MacLeod, M. and Barter, C. (1988) *We Know it's Tough to Talk: Boys in Need of Help*. London: Childline.

Maclure, M., Phillips, T. and Wilkinson, A. (1988) *Oracy Matters*. Milton Keynes: Open University Press.

Maher, C. (1982) 'Behavioral effects of using conduct problem adolescents as cross-age tutors'. *Psychology in the Schools*, 19, 360–64.

Mallick, S. and Candless, B. (1966) 'A study of catharsis aggression'. *Journal of Personality and Social Psychology*, 4, 591–6.

Marchant, S. (1995) 'The essential curriculum for pupils exhibiting emotional and behaviour difficulties'. *Therapeutic Care and Education*, 4, 36–47.

Marmot, M., Bosma, H., Hemingway, H., Brunner, E. and Stanfield, S. (1997) 'Contribution of job control and other risk factors to social variations in coronary heart disease incidence'. *Lancet*, 350, 235–9.

Marshall, H. and Weinstein, R. (1984) 'Classroom factors affecting students' self-evaluation: an interactional model'. *Review of Educational Research*, 54, 301–25.

Maslow, A. (1970) *Motivation and Personality*, 2nd edn. New York: Harper and Row.

Mayer, J. and Salovey, P. (1993) 'The intelligence of emotional intelligence'. *Intelligence*, 17, 433–42.

Mayer, J. and Salovey, P. (1997) 'What is emotional intelligence?' In P. Salovey and S. Sluyter (eds) *Emotional Development and Emotional Intelligence*. New York: Basic Books.

McCallum, R. and Bracken, B. (1993) 'Interpersonal relations between school children and their peers, parents and teachers'. *Educational Psychology Review*, 5, 155–76.

McCarthy, K. (1998) *Learning by Heart: the Role of Emotional Education in Raising School Achievement*. Brighton: Re:membering Education.

McCord, J. and Tremblay, R.E. (1992) *Preventing Antisocial Behaviour*. New York; London: The Guilford Press.

McDonald, H. and Ziglio, E. (1994) 'European schools in a changing environment: health promotion opportunities not to be lost'. C. Chu and R. Simpson (eds) *Ecological Public Health: From Vision to Practice*, Brisbane: Griffiths University.

McEwen, A. and Thompson, W. (1997) 'After the national curriculum: teacher stress and morale'. *Research in Education*, 57, 57–66.

McGinnis, E. (1990) *Skillstreaming in Early Childhood: Teaching Prosocial Skills to the Preschool and Kindergarten Child*. Champaign, IL: Research Press.

McGinnis, E. (1984) *Skillstreaming the Elementary School Child: A Guide for Teaching Prosocial Skills*. Champaign, IL: Research Press.

McKenzie, J. and Williams, I. (1982) 'Are your students learning in a safe environment?' *Journal of School Health*, 52, 284–85.

McMillan, J. (1992) *A Qualitative Study of Resilient At-Risk Students: Review of Literature*. Virginia: Metropolitan Educational Research Consortium.

McNeely, D. (1987) *Touching – Body Therapy and Depth Psychology*. Toronto: Inner City Books.

McWhirter, J. and Wetton, N. (1995) *European Network of Health Promoting Schools: Centralised Support Seminars*. Southampton: Health Education Unit, University of Southampton.

Mental Health Foundation (1999) *The Big Picture: Promoting Children and Young People's Mental Health*. London: The Mental Health Foundation.

Meridian Broadcasting Charitable Trust (1998) *Talking About It*. Southampton: Resources Base, Meridian Television.

Metcalfe, O., Weare, K., Williams, M. and Young, I. (1993) *Promoting the Health of Young People in Europe*. Copenhagen: European Community and WHO.

Middleton, M. and Cartledge, G. (1995) 'The effects of social skills instruction and parental involvement on the aggressive behaviors of African American males'. *Behavior Modification*, 19, 192–210.

Miller, W. and Rollnick, S. (1991) *Motivational Interviewing: Preparing People for Change*. New York: Guildford Press.

Mind (1997) *The Bird and the Word: Materials for Mental Health Education in Secondary Schools*. London: Mind.

Mischel, W. and Peake, P. (1990) 'Predicting adolescent cognitive and self-regulatory competences from pre-school delay of gratification'. *Developmental Psychology*, 26 (6), 978–86.

Mitchell, J. (1984) *What's to be Done About Illness and Health?* Harmondsworth: Penguin.

Mize, J. and Ladd, G. (1990) 'A cognitive–social learning approach to social skill training with low status preschool children'. *Developmental Psychology*, 26 (3), 388–97.

Moon, A. (1996) *Skills for the Primary School Child*. Manchester: TACADE.

Moos, R. (1991) 'Connections between school, work and family settings'. B. Fraser and H. Walberg (eds) *Educational Environments*. Oxford: Pergamon.

Morgan, S. (1983) 'Development of empathy in emotionally disturbed children'. *Journal of Humanistic Education and Development*, 22, 70–79.

Morris, S. (1982) 'A classroom group process for behavior change'. *Pointer*, 26, 25–28.

Morton, L. (1993) 'Interpersonal skill development through cooperative education'. *Guidance and Counselling*, 9, 26–31.

Mosley, J. (1996) *Quality Circle Time*. Cambridge: LDA.

Mosley, J. (1993) *Turn Your School Round*. Cambridge: LDA.

Nastasi, B. and Clements, D. (1991) 'Research on cooperative learning: implications for practice'. *School Psychology Review*, 20 (1), 110–31.

Neilans, T. and Israel, A. (1981) 'Towards maintenance and generalization of behavior change: Teaching children self-regulation and self-instructional skills'. *Cognitive Therapy and Research*, 5, 189–95.

Nelson, C. (1987) 'Behavioral interventions: what works and what doesn't'. *Pointer*, 31, 45–50.

Nelson, J., Smith, D., Young, R. and Dodd, J. (1991) 'A review of self-management outcome research conducted with students who exhibit behavioral disorders'. *Behavioral Disorders*, 16, 169–79.

Nelson Jones, R. (1993) *Human Relationship Skills*. London: Cassell.

Nelson Jones, R. (1989) *Effective Thinking Skills: Preventing and Managing Personal Problems*. London: Cassell.

New Policy Institute (1998) *Second Chances: Exclusion from School and Equality of Opportunity*. London: New Policy Institute.

NFER (1995) *The Health Promoting School: A Baseline Survey*. London: HEA.

Ninness, H. (1995) 'The effect of a self-management training package on the transfer of aggression control procedures in the absence of supervision'. *Behavior Modification*, 19 (4 October), 464–90.

Nowicki, S. and Duke, M. (1992) *Helping the Child Who Doesn't Fit In*. Atlanta: Peachtree Publishers.

Nutbeam, D., Haglund, B., Farley, P. and Tillgren, P. (1991) *Youth Health Promotion: From Theory to Practice in School and Community*. London: Forbes.

Nutbeam, D. (1992) 'The health promoting school: closing the gap between theory and practice'. *Health Promotion International*, 9, 39–47.

O'Donnell, J., Hawkins, J., Catalano, R., Abbott, R. and Day, E. (1995) 'Preventing school failure, drug use and delinquency among low income children'. *American Journal of Orthopsychiatry*, 65, 87–99.

Ollech, D. (1992) 'Anger control for adolescents: review of social skills and cognitive behavioral interventions'. I. Fodor (ed.) *Adolescent Assertiveness and Social Skills Training: A Clinical Handbook*. New York: Springer.

Olweus, D. (1995) 'Bullying or peer abuse at school: facts and interventions'. *Current Directions in Psychological Science*, 4, 196–200.

Oppenheim, A. (1996) *Questionnaire Design, Interviewing and Attitude Measurement*. London: Pinter.

Palardy, J. (1992) 'Behavior modification: it does work, but … '. *Journal of Instructional Psychology*, 19, 127–31.

Palardy, J. (1995) 'Dealing with misbehavior: two approaches'. *Journal of Instructional Psychology*, 22, 135–40.

Parsons, C., Stears, D., Thomas, C., Thomas, L. and Holland, J. (1997) *The Implementation of the ENHPS in Different National Contexts*. Canterbury: Centre for Health Education and Research, Canterbury Christ Church College.

Pattenden, J. (1998) 'Development of indicators for the ENHPS'. Paper presented at the First Workshop for the Evaluation of the Health Promoting School, Thun, Switzerland. Copenhagen: WHO.

Patterson, L. and Burns, J. (1990) *Women, Assertiveness and Health*. London: HEA.

Pease, A. (1981) *Body Language: How to Read Others' Thoughts by their Gestures*. Sydney: Camel.

Peatfield, Z. (1998) 'Social exclusion'. *Young Minds*, 34, 8.

Perkins, E., Simnet, I. and Wright, L. (1999) *Evidence Based Health Promotion*. Chichester: John Wiley.

Perry, B. (1996) *Maltreated Children: Experience, Brain Development and the Next Generation*. New York: Norton.

Peterson, A., Sarigiani, P. and Kennedy, R. (1991) 'Adolescent depression: why more girls?' *Journal of Youth and Adolescence*, 20. 247–72.

Petersen, L. (1992) 'Stop–Think–Do: a systems based pro-social skills training program'. *Guidance and Counselling*, 8, 24–35.

Phares, J.E. (1976) *Locus of Control in Personality*. New Jersey: General Learning Press.

Piaget, J. and Inhelder, B. (1958) *The Growth of Logical Thinking from Childhood to Adolescence*. London: Routledge.

Piette, D. (ed.) (1995) *Towards an Evaluation of the European Network of Health Promoting Schools*. Copenhagen: WHO (with the European Commission, the Council of Europe and the Universite Libre de Bruxelles).

Polirstok, S. (1986) 'Training problematic adolescents as peer tutors: benefits for the tutor and the school at large'. *Techniques*, 2, 204–10.

Pollack, P. (1991) *Kids in Action: A Community Development Approach to Children's Health*. Toronto: Lawrence Heights Community Health Centre Press.

Potel, D. and Bowley, J. (1998) 'Working together in schools: the Southwark Adolescent Schools Initiative'. *Young Minds*, 37, 12–14.

Powell, K., Muir Mcclain, L. and Halasyamani, L. (1995) 'A review of selected school-based conflict-resolution and peer mediation projects'. *Journal of School Health*, 65 (10), 426–31.

Powell, S. (1993) 'The power of positive peer influence: leadership training for today's teens'. *Special Services in the Schools*, 8 (1), 119–36.

Rigby, K. (1996) *Bullying in Schools*. London: Jessica Kingsley.

Roberts, D. (1997) 'Developmental groupwork: encouraging skills in self-expression for pupils with emotional and behavioural difficulties'. *Educational Psychology in Practice*, 13 (2), 122–9.

Robinson, G. and Maines, B. (1997) *Crying for Help: the No Blame Approach to Bullying*. Bristol: Lucky Duck Publishing.

Robinson, P. (1967) *Education and Poverty*. London: Methuen.

Rodmell, S. and Watt, A. (eds) (1986) *The Politics of Health Education*. London: Routledge.

Rogers, A. (1996) *Teaching Adults*. 2nd edn. Buckingham: Open University.

Rogers, B. (1994) *Behaviour Recovery: A Whole-School Program for Mainstream Schools*. Melbourne, Victoria: Australian Council for Educational Research.

Rogers C. (1983) *Freedom to Learn for the 1980s*. Ohio: Charles E Merril.

Rogers, C. (1978) *Carl Rogers on Personal Power*. London: Constable.

Rogers, C. (1961) *On Becoming a Person*. London: Constable.

Rollinson, R. (1992) 'Myths we work by'. *Theraputic Care and Education*, 10, (1) 3–82.

Ronen, T. (1994) 'Imparting self-control skills in the school setting'. *Child and Family Behavior Therapy*, 16 (1), 1–20.

Rosenthal, H. (1993) 'Friendship groups: an approach to helping friendless children'. *Educational Psychology in Practice*, 9 (July), 112–20.

Rosenthal, R. and Jacobson, L. (1968) *Pygmalion in the Classroom*. New York: Rhineheart and Winston.

Roswal, E. (1995) 'Effects of collaborative peer tutoring on urban 7th graders'. *Journal of Educational Research*, 88 (5), 275–79.

Rowe, D. (1996) *Depression, the Way Out of Your Prison*. London: Routledge.

Rowling, L. (1996) 'The adaptability of the health promoting schools concept: a case study from Australia. *Health Education Research*, 11, (4) 519–26.

Rutter, M., Maughan, B., Mortimore, P. and Ouston, J. (1979) *Fifteen Thousand Hours: Secondary Schools and their Effects on Children*. Cambridge, MA: Harvard University Press.

Rutter, M., Hagel, A. and Giller, H. (1998) *Anti-social Behaviour and Young People*. Cambridge: Cambridge University Press.

Ryder and Campbell (1988) *Balancing Acts in Personal, Social and Health Education*. London: Routledge.

Saarni, C. (1997) 'Emotional competence and self-regulation in childhood'. P. Salovey and S. Sluyter (eds) *Emotional Development and Emotional Intelligence: Implications for Educators*. New York: Basic Books.

Salend, S. and Sonnenschein, P. (1989) 'Validating the effectiveness of a cooperative learning strategy through direct observation'. *Journal of School Psychology*, 27, 47–58.

Salmon, P. (1988) *Psychology for Teachers: An Alternative Approach*. London: Hutchinson.

Salovey, P. and Sluyter, D. (eds) (1997) *Emotional Development and Emotional Intelligence*. New York: Basic Books.

Sanders, P. and Swinden, L. (1990) *Knowing Me: Knowing You: Strategies for Sex Education in the Primary School*. Cambridge: LDA.

Sarros, J. and Sarros, A. (1992) 'Social support and teacher burnout'. *Journal of Educational Administration*, 30 (1) 55–69.

Schaps, E., Lewis, C. and Watson, M. (1996) 'Building community in school'. *Principal*, November 1996, 29–31.

Scruggs, T., Mastropieri, M. and Richter, L. (1985) 'Peer tutoring with behaviorally disordered students: social and academic benefits'. *Behavioral Disorders*, 10, 283–94.

Secker, J. (1998) 'Current conceptualizations of mental health and mental health promotion'. *Health Education Research*, 13 (1), 57–66.

Seligman, M. (1991) *Learned Optimism*. Milson's Point, Australia: Random House.

Seligman, M. (1975) *Helplessness: On Depression, Development and Death*. Reading: Freeman.

Seyle, H. (1974) *Stress Without Distress*. Sevenoaks: Hodder and Stoughton.

Shamoo, T.K. and Patros, P.G. (1990) *Helping Your Child Cope with Depression and Suicidal Thoughts*. San Francisco: Jossey-Bass.

Shaw, J. and Riskind, J. (1983) 'Predicting job stress using data from the position analysis questionnaire'. *Journal of Applied Psychology*, 68, 253–61.

Shendell, M. (1992) 'Communication training for adolescent girls in junior high school setting: learning to take risks in self-expression'. I. Fodor (ed.) *Adolescent Assertiveness and Social Skills Training: A Clinical Handbook*. New York: Springer.

Shriver, T. and Weissberg, R. (1998) 'No new wars: prevention should be a comprehensive strategy, not a fad'. *Casel Collections*, vol. 1, edn 1.5. Chicago, IL: The Collaborative for the Advancement of Social and Emotional Learning (CASEL).

Slaby, R. and Guerra, N. (1988) 'Cognitive mediations of aggression in adolescent offenders'. *Developmental Psychology* (24), 580–8.

Smith, D. (1995) 'Youth crime and conduct disorders: trends, patterns and causal explanations'. M. Rutter and D. Smith (eds) *Psychosocial Disorders in Young People*. Chichester: John Wiley.

Smith, M. (1975) *When I Say No I Feel Guilty*. London: The Dial Press.

Smith, R. (1998) *No Lessons Learnt*. London: The Children's Society.

Solomon, D., Watson, M., Battistich, V., Schaps, E. and Delucchi, K. (1992) 'Creating a caring community: a school based programme to promote children's prosocial competence'. E. Oser, J. Patty and A. Dick (eds) *Effective and Responsible Teaching*. San Francisco: Jossey-Bass.

Sotto, E. (1994) *When Teaching Becomes Learning*. London: Cassell.

Springett, J. (1999) *Practical Advice on Evaluating Health Promotion*. Copenhagen: WHO Regional Office for Europe, Working Group on Health Promotion Evaluation.

St Leger, L. (1999) 'The health promoting primary school'. *Health Education Research*, 14 (1), 51–69.

Stacey, H. and Robinson, P. (1997) *Let's Mediate*. Bristol: Lucky Duck Publishing.

Stanford, L. and Donovan, M. (1993) *Women and Self-Esteem*. Harmondsworth: Penguin.

Stanford, G. (1995) *Developing Effective Classroom Groups: British Edition*. P. Stoate (ed.). Bristol: E.G. Brown.

Stears, D., Clift, S. and Blackman, S. (1995) 'Health, sex and drugs education: rhetoric and realities'. J. Ahier and A. Ross (eds) *The Social Subjects Within the Curriculum*. Lewes: Falmer.

Steiner, C. (1984) 'Emotional literacy'. *Transactional Analysis Journal*, 14, 162–73.

Steiner, C. (1999) *Achieving Emotional Literacy*. London: Bloomsbury.

Stewart, C. and Lewis, W. (1986) 'Effects of assertiveness training on the self-esteem of black high-school students. *Journal of Counseling and Development*, 64, (10), 638–41.

Stewart-Brown, S. (1998) *Evaluating Health Promotion in Schools: Reflections From the UK*. Oxford: Health Services Research Unit, Department of Public Health, University of Oxford.

Sylwester, R. (1995) *A Celebration of Neurons: An Educator's Guide to the Human Brain*. Alexandria, Vancover: ASCD.

TACADE (1996) *Skills for Adolescence*. Manchester: TACADE.

Tattum, D.P. and Lane, D.A. (eds) (1989) *Bullying in Schools*. Stoke-on-Trent: Trentham Books.

Taylor, W. and Hoedt, K. (1974) 'Classroom-related behavior problems: counsel parents, teachers, or children?' *Journal of Counseling Psychology*, 2, 3–8.

Thomas, S. (1993) 'Education reform: juggling the concepts of equality and elitism'. Evans, J. (1993) *Equality, Education and Physical Education*, Falmer: Brighton.

Thurlow, M. (1995) *Staying in School: Strategies for Middle School Students with Learning & Emotional Disabilities. ABC Dropout Prevention and Intervention Series*. Minneapolis: Institute on Community Integration, University of Minnesota.

Tierney, J. (1993) 'Empowering aggressive youth to change'. *Journal of Emotional and Behavioral Problems*, 2, 41–5.

Tilford, S., Delaney, F. and Vogels, M. (1997) *Effectiveness of Mental Health Promotion Interventions*. London: HEA.

Tobler, N. and Stratton, H. (1997) 'Effectiveness of school-based drug prevention programs: a meta-analysis of the research'. *Journal of Primary Prevention*, 18 (1), 71–128.

Tones, K. (1986) 'Health education and the ideology of health promotion: a review of alternative strategies'. *Health Education Research: Theory and Practice*, 1 (1), 3–12.

Tones, K. (1981) 'Health education: prevention or subversion?' *Royal Society of Health Journal*, 101 (3), 114–17.

Tones, K. and Tilford, S. (1994) *Health Education, Effectiveness, Efficiency and Equity)*, 2nd edn. London: Chapman and Hall.

Townsend, P., Whitehead, M. and Davidson, N. (1992) *Inequalities in Health*. Harmondsworth: Penguin.

Trelawney-Ross, D. (1988) 'Helping students respond meaningfully to poetry as well as pass exams'. *English in Education*, 32 (1), 45–54.

Trent, R. (1992) 'Breaking the single continuum'. D. Trent (ed.) *Promotion of Mental Health, Volume 1*. Aldershot: Avebury.

Troyna, B. (1993) *Racism and Education*. Milton Keynes: Open University

Tudor, K. (1996) *Mental Health Promotion*. London: Routledge.

Tudge, C (1998) 'A drug free state just isn't normal'. *New Statesman*, January 9, 24–25.

Tuettemann, E. and Punch, K. (1992) 'Teachers' psychological distress: the ameliorating effects of control over the work environment'. *Educational Review*, 44 (2), 181–94.

Tunstall, D. (1994) *Social Competence Needs in Young Children: What the Research Says*. Paper presented at the Association for Childhood Education International Study Conference, New Orleans, 30 March – 2 April 1994.

US Government General Accounting Office (1995) *School Safety: Promising Initiatives for Addressing School Violence. Report to the Ranking Minority Member, Subcommittee on Children and Families, Committee on Labor and Human Resources. US Senate*. Washington, DC: General Accounting Office.

Valliant, G.E. (1977) *Adaptation to Life*. Boston: Little Brown.

Vaughan, S. and Lancelotta, G. (1990) 'Teaching interpersonal social skills to poorly accepted students: peer-pairing versus non-peer-pairing'. *Journal of School Psychology*, 28, 181–88.

Veen, C. (1995) *Evaluation of the IUHPE Project on the Effectiveness of Health Promotion and Health Education* (12 volumes). Utrecht, The Netherlands: Dutch Health Education Centre.

Walberg, H.J. (1984) 'Families as partners in educational productivity'. *Phi Delta Kappan*, 84 (6), 397–400.

Walker, H. (1995) *Antisocial Behavior in School: Strategies and Best Practices*. Pacific Grove, CA: Brooks/Cole Publishing.

Wallston, K.A. and Wallston, B.S. (1982) 'Who is responsible for our health? The construct of health locus of control'. In G.S. Sanders and J. Suls (eds) *Social Psychology of Health and Illness*. New Jersey: Erlbaum Associates.

Walsh, R. (1990) 'A creative arts program in social skills training for early adolescents – an exploratory study. *Arts in Psychotherapy*, 17 (2), 131–7.

Walsh-Bowers, R. (1992) 'A creative drama prevention program for easing early adolescents' adjustment to school transitions'. *Journal of Primary Prevention*, 13, 131–47.

Watson, O. (1972) *Proxemic Behavior: A Cross Cultural Study*. The Hague: Mowton.

Watson, D.L. and Tharp, R.G. (1985) *Self Directed Behaviour: Self Modification for Personal Adjustment*, 4th edn. Monterey, CA: Brooks/Cole.

Weare, K. (1992) 'The contribution of education to health promotion'. R. Bunton and G. Macdonald (eds) *Health Promotion: Disciplines and Diversity*. London: Routledge.

Weare, K. and Gray, G. (1994) *Promoting Mental and Emotional Health in the European Network of Health Promoting Schools*. Copenhagen: WHO Regional Office for Europe.

Webber, J., Scheuermann, B., McCall, C. and Coleman, M. (1993) 'Research on self-monitoring as a behavior management technique in special-education classrooms – a descriptive review'. *Remedial and Special Education*, 14 (2), 38–56.

Weiler, R. and Dorman, S. (1995) 'The role of school health instruction in preventing interpersonal violence'. *Educational Psychology Review*, 7, 69–91.

Weissberg, R. and Elias, M. (1993) 'Enhancing young people's social competence and health behaviour: An important challenge for educators, scientists, policy-makers and funders'. *Applied & Preventive Psychology*, 3, 179–90.

Weissberg, R.P. and Greenberg, M. (1997) 'Social and community competence-enhancement and prevention programmes'. W. Damon (ed.) *Handbook of Child Psychology: Vol 4, Child Psychology in Practice*. New York: John Wiley.

Wetton, N. and Cansell, P. (1993) *Feeling Good: Raising Self-Esteem in the Primary School Classroom*. London: Forbes.

Wetton, N. and McCoy, M. (1998) *Confidence to Learn: A Guide to Extending Health Education in the Primary School*. Edinburgh: Health Education Board for Scotland.

WHO (1999) *Health Behaviour in School Age Children Questionnaire*. Copenhagen: WHO Regional Office for Europe.

WHO (1998a) *WHO's Global School Health Initiative: Health Promoting Schools*. Geneva: WHO.

WHO (1998b) *Health Promotion Evaluation: Recommendations to Policy Makers. Report of the WHO European Working Group on Health Promotion Evaluation*. Copenhagen: WHO Regional Office for Europe.

WHO (1998c) *Violence Prevention: An Important Element of a Health Promoting School: WHO Information Series on School Health, Document 3*. Geneva: WHO.

WHO (1997a) *The Health Promoting School: an Investment in Education, Health and Democracy: Conference Report on the First Conference of the European Network of Health Promoting Schools, Thessaloniki, Greece*. Copenhagen: WHO Regional Office for Europe.

WHO (1997b) *The Health Promoting School: an Investment in Education, Health and Democracy: Case Study Book. First Conference of the European Network of Health Promoting Schools, Thessaloniki, Greece*. Copenhagen: WHO Regional Office for Europe.

WHO (1996) *School Health Promotion – Series 5: Regional Guidelines: Development of Health Promoting Schools: A Framework for Action*. Manila: WHO.

WHO (1994) *Life Skills Education in Schools: Introduction and Guidelines to Facilitate the Development and Implementation of Life Skills Programmes*. Geneva: WHO Division of Mental Health and Prevention of Substance Abuse.

WHO (1991) *Sundsvall Statement on Supportive Environments for Health*. Copenhagen: World Health Organistion Regional Office for Europe.

WHO (1986) *Ottawa Charter For Health Promotion*. Geneva: WHO.

WHO (1985) *Targets For Health For All – Targets in Support of European Regional Strategy for Health For All*. Geneva: WHO.

WHO (1946) *Constitution*. Geneva: WHO.

WHO, CEC and CE (1993) *The European Network of Health Promoting Schools: Resource Manual*. Copenhagen: WHO Regional Office for Europe.

White, S. (1995) *Confidentiality in Schools: A Training Manual*. London: Brook Advisory Centres.

Wilberg, P. (1998) *The Little Black Book of Negative Thinking: A Philosophical Approach to Depression*. London: Third Ear.

Wilkins, C. (1999) *Making 'Good Citizens': the Social and Political Attitudes of PGCE Students*. London: Carfax.

Williams, R. (1989) *The Trusting Heart*. New York: Random House.

Williams, T., Wetton, N. and Moon, A. (1992a) *A Picture of Health: What Do You Do That Makes You Healthy and Keeps You Healthy?* London: HEA.

Williams, T., Wetton, N. and Moon, A. (1992b) *A Way In: Five Key Areas of Health Education*. London: HEA.

Willis, P. (1977) *Learning to Labour*. Aldershot: Gower.

Winnicott, D. (1984) *The Maturational Process and the Facilitating Environment*. London: Hogarth.

Winnicott, D. (1974) *Playing and Reality*. London: Pelican.

Winnicott, D. (1964) *The Child, the Family and the Outside World*. Harmondsworth: Penguin.

Withers, G. (1995) *Programs for At-Risk Youth: A Review of the American, Canadian and British Literature since 1984*. ACER Research Monograph No. 47. Melbourne: The Australian Council for Educational Research.

Wolfelt, A. (1983) *Helping Children Cope with Grief*. New York: Accelerated Development.

Women in Theatre (1996) *Drama in Health Promotion*. Birmingham: West Midlands Arts, Birmingham City Council.

Wood, D. (1992) 'Teaching talk'. K. Norman (ed.) *Thinking Voices: the Work of the National Curriculum Project*. London: Hodder and Stoughton.

Wubbels, T., Brekelmans, M. and Hoodmayers, H. (1991) 'Interpersonal teacher behaviour in the classroom'. B. Fraser and H. Walberg (eds) *Educational Environments*. Oxford: Pergamon.

Wulf, M. (1993) 'Is your child suffering from sick building syndrome?' *PTA Today*, 19, 12–13.

Wylie, R. (1961) *The Self Concept*. Nebraska: University of Nebraska Press.

Yell, M. (1988) 'The effects of jogging on the rates of selected target behaviors of behaviorally disordered students'. *Behavioral Disorders*, 13, 273–79.

Young, I. and Williams, T. (1989) *The Healthy School*. Edinburgh: Scottish Health Education Group.

Young, M. (1971) 'An approach to the study of curricula as socially organised knowledge'. M. Young (ed.) *Knowledge and Control*. West Drayton, Middlesex: Collier Macmillan.

Zaragoza, N., Vaughan, S. and McIntosh, R. (1991) 'Social skills interventions and children with behavior problems: a review'. *Behavioral Disorders*, 16, 260–75.

Index